Large Print

SENIORS

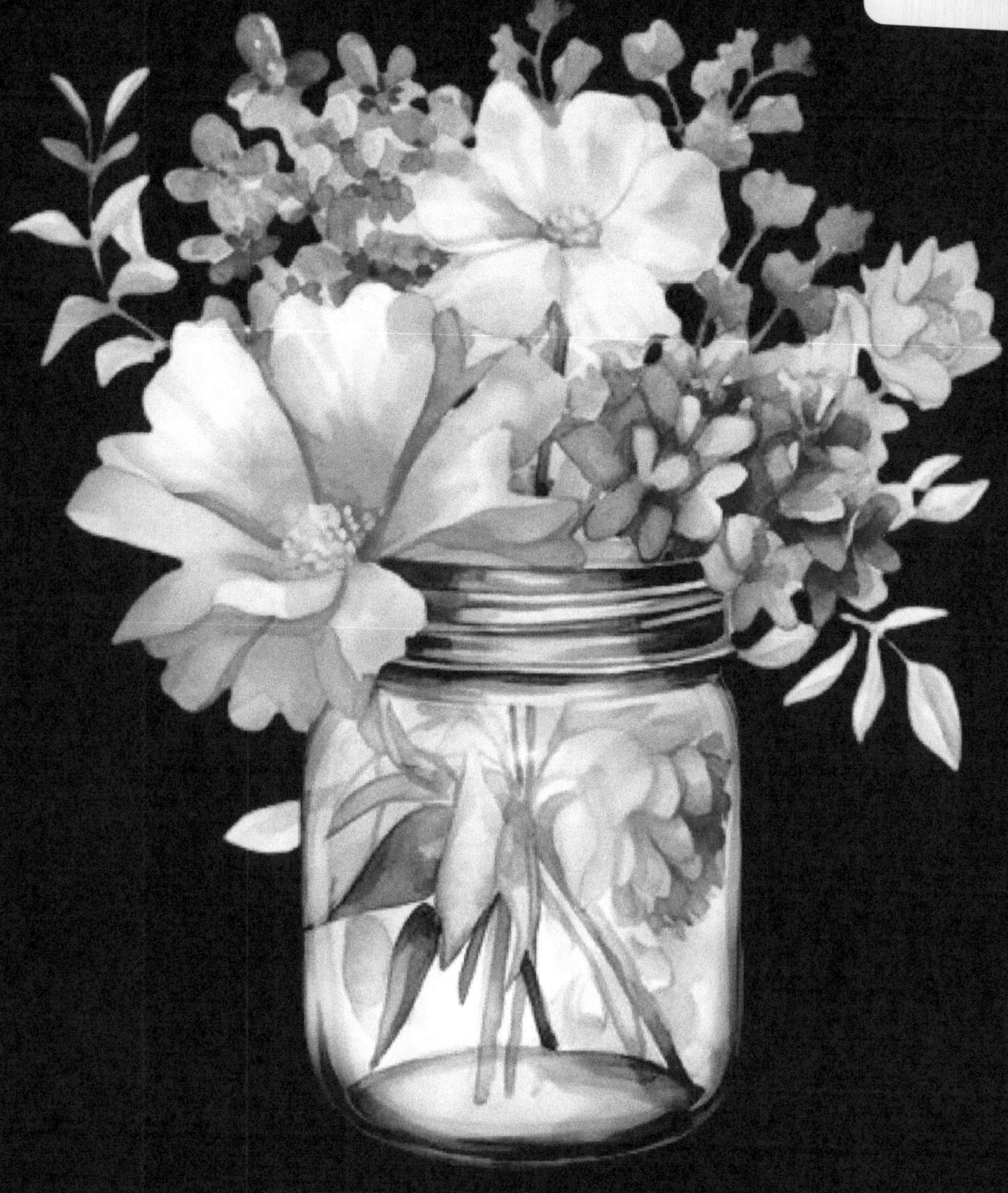

Simple Coloring Book

this book belongs to

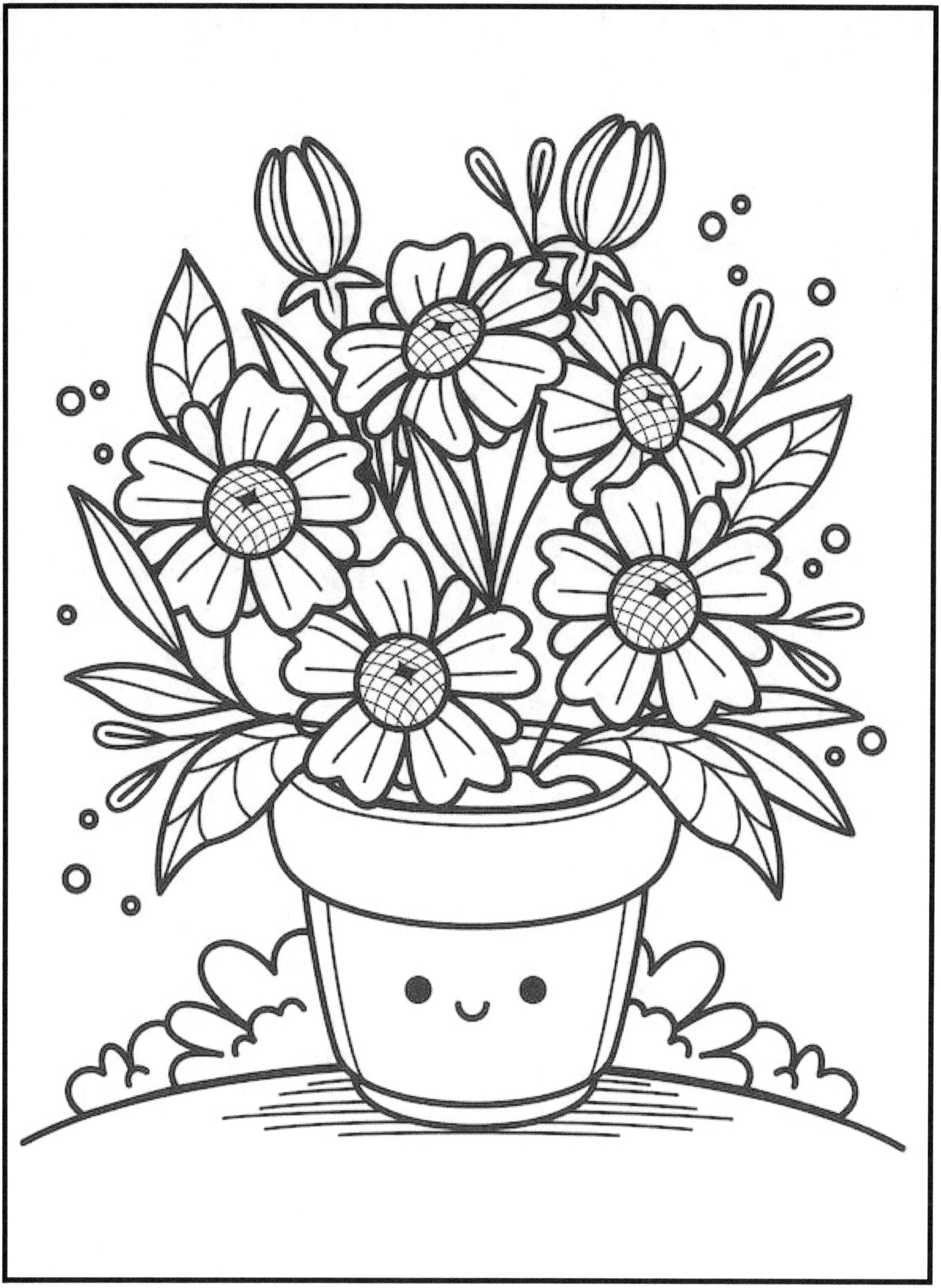

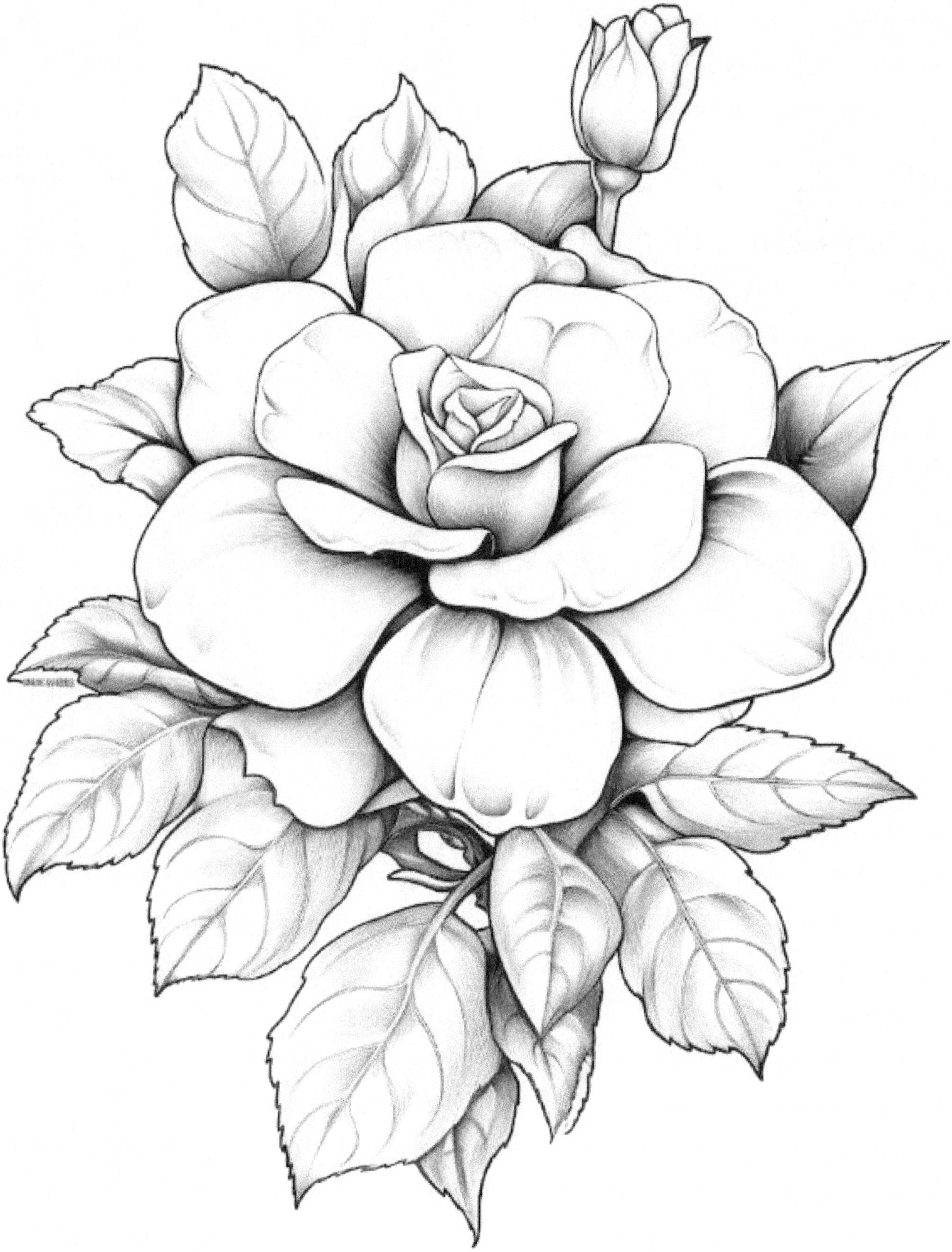

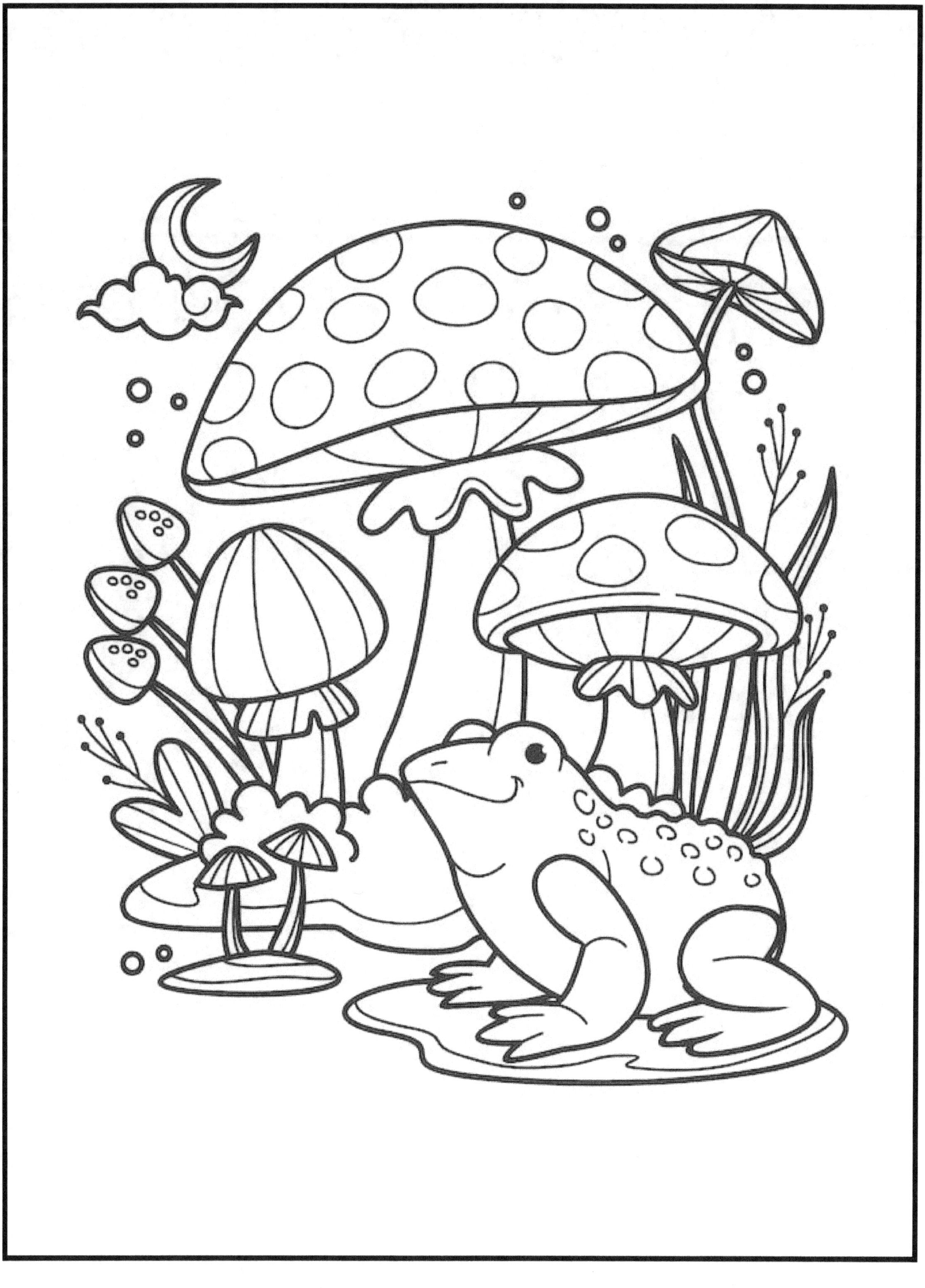

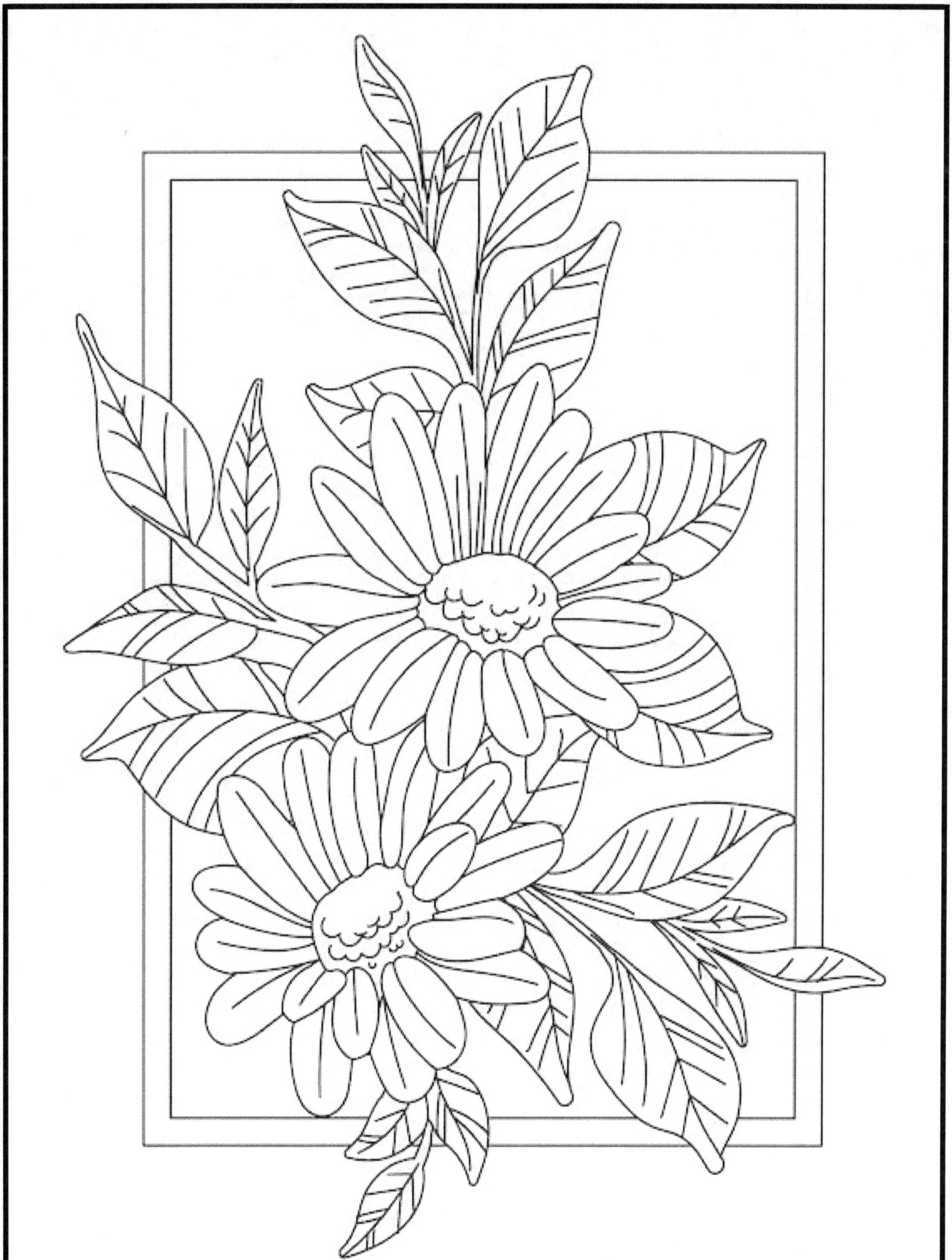

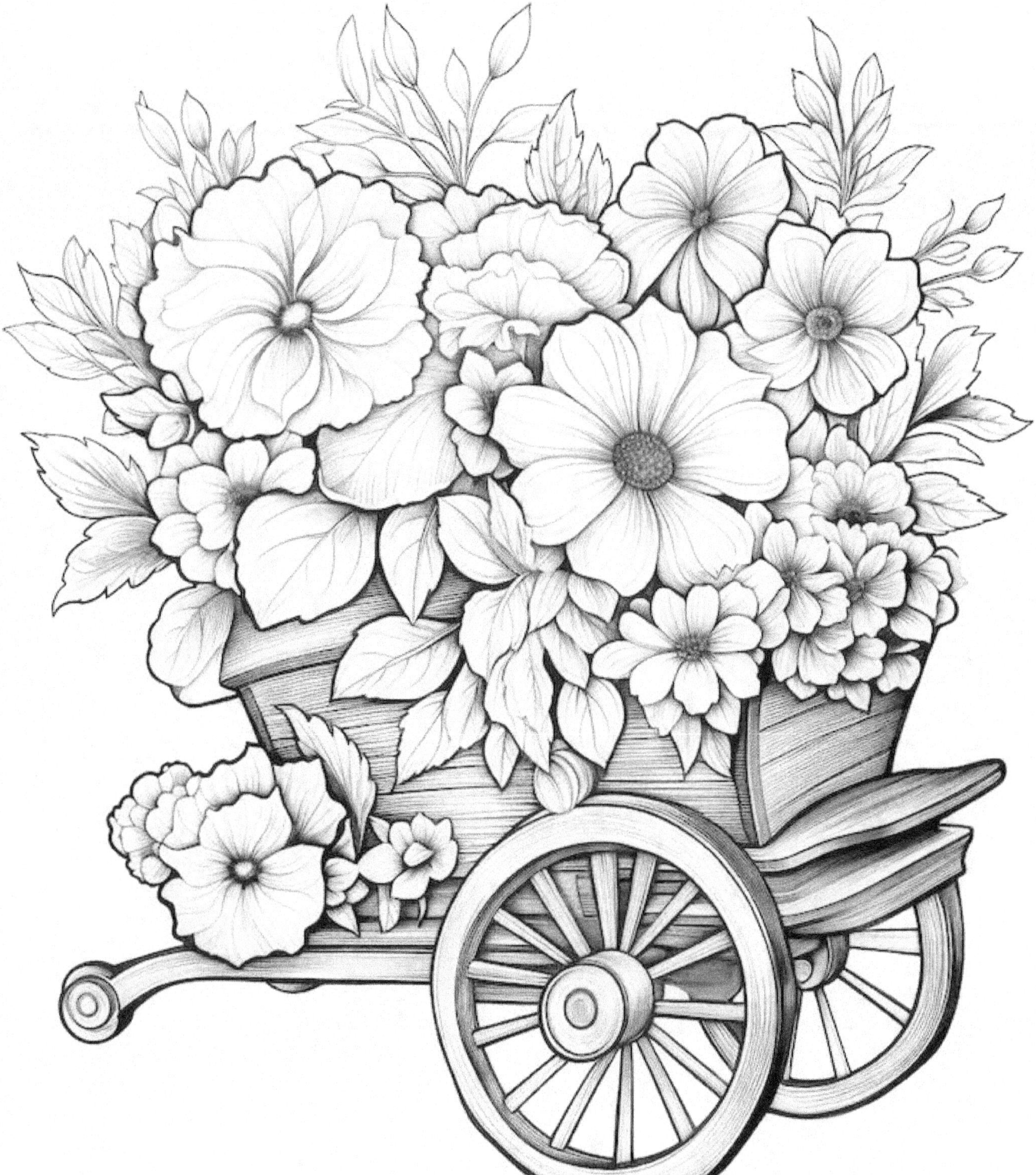

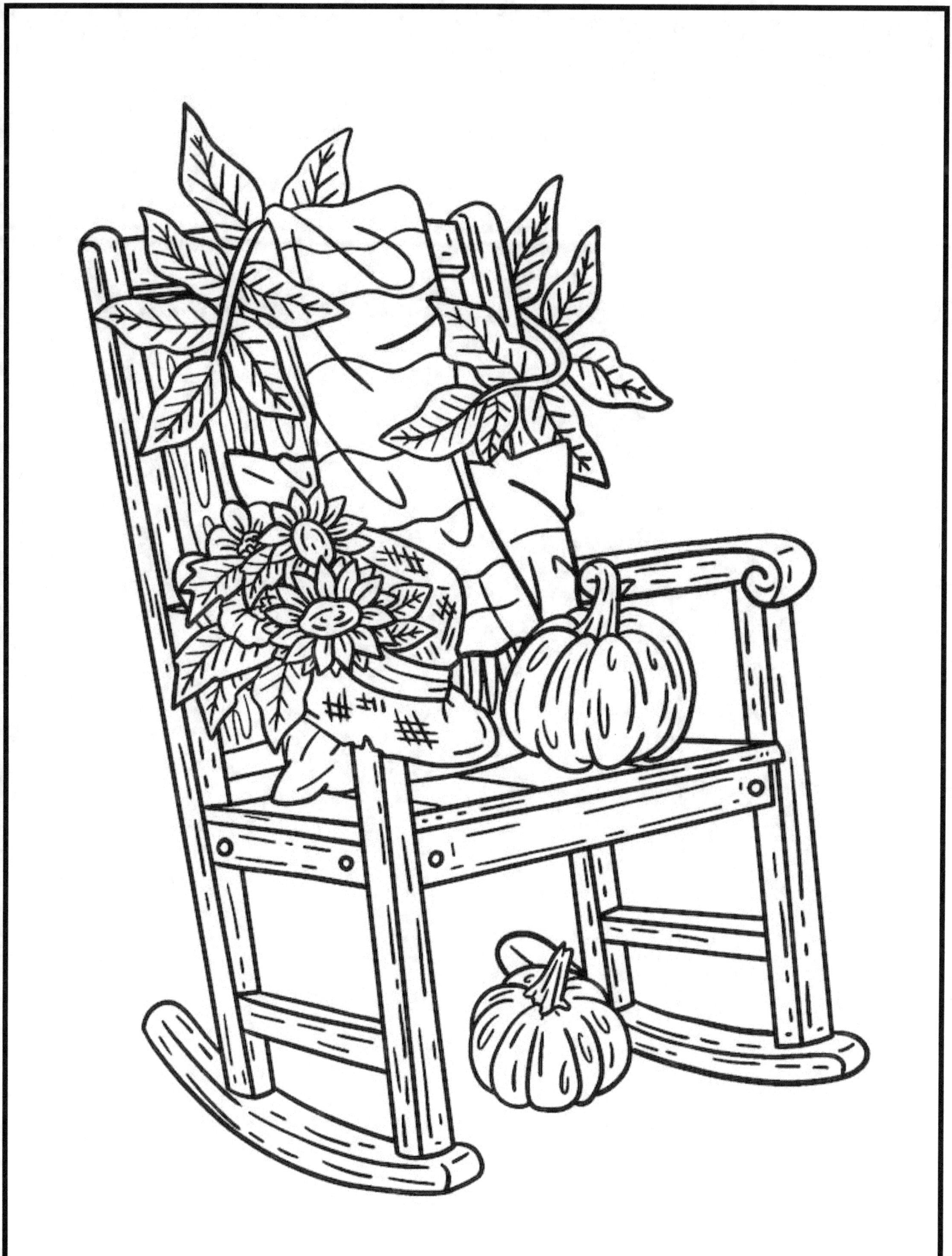

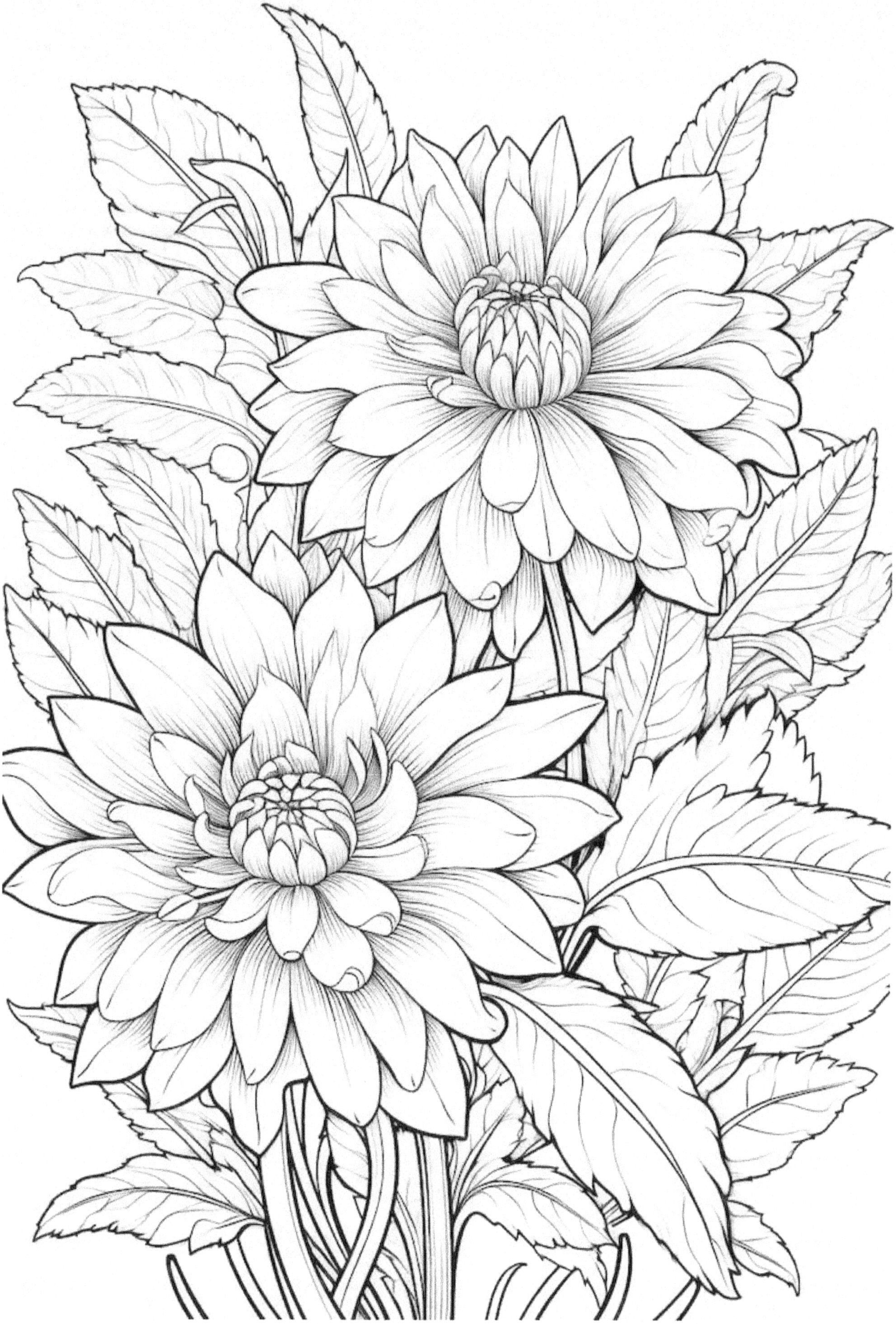

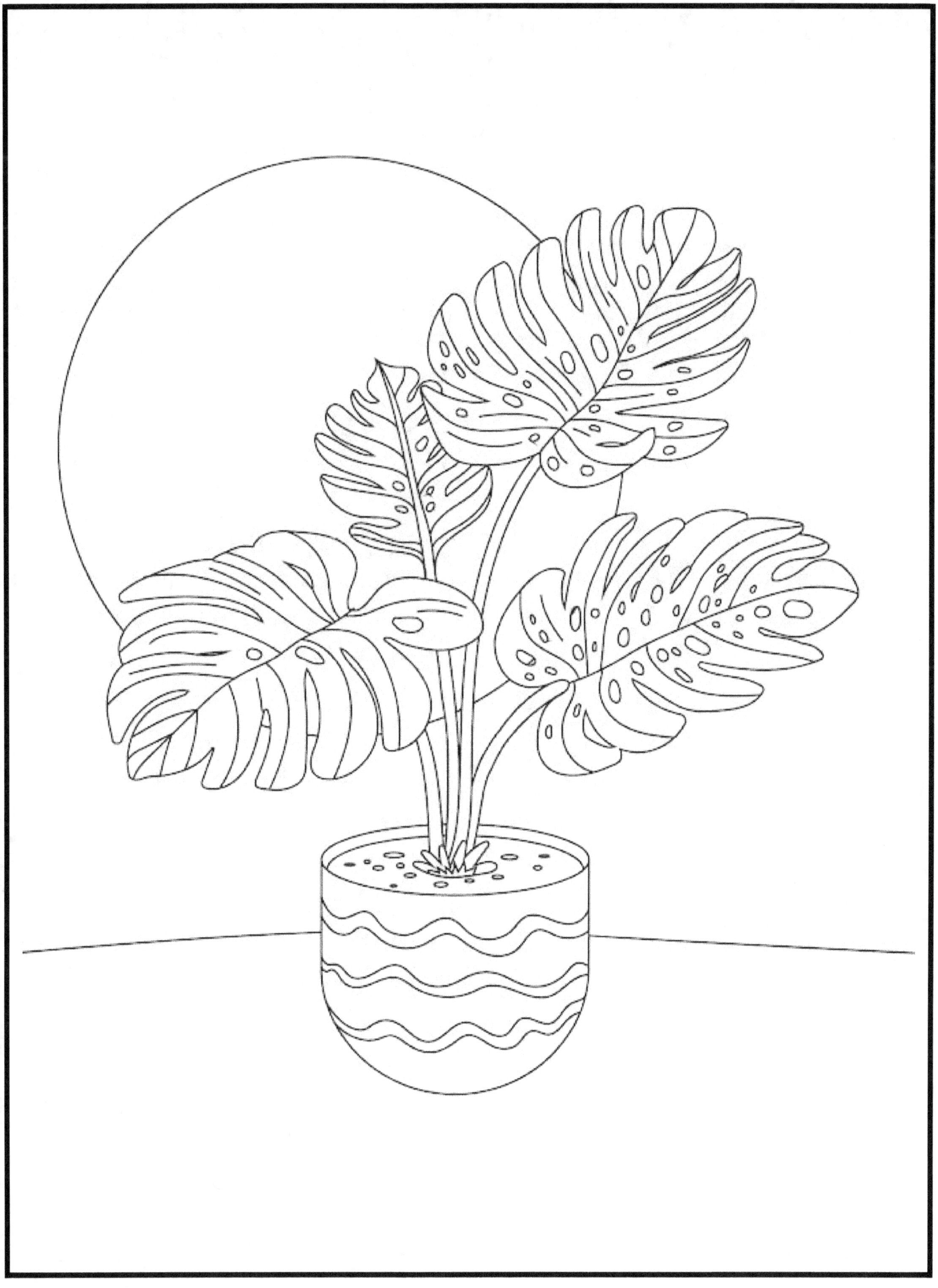

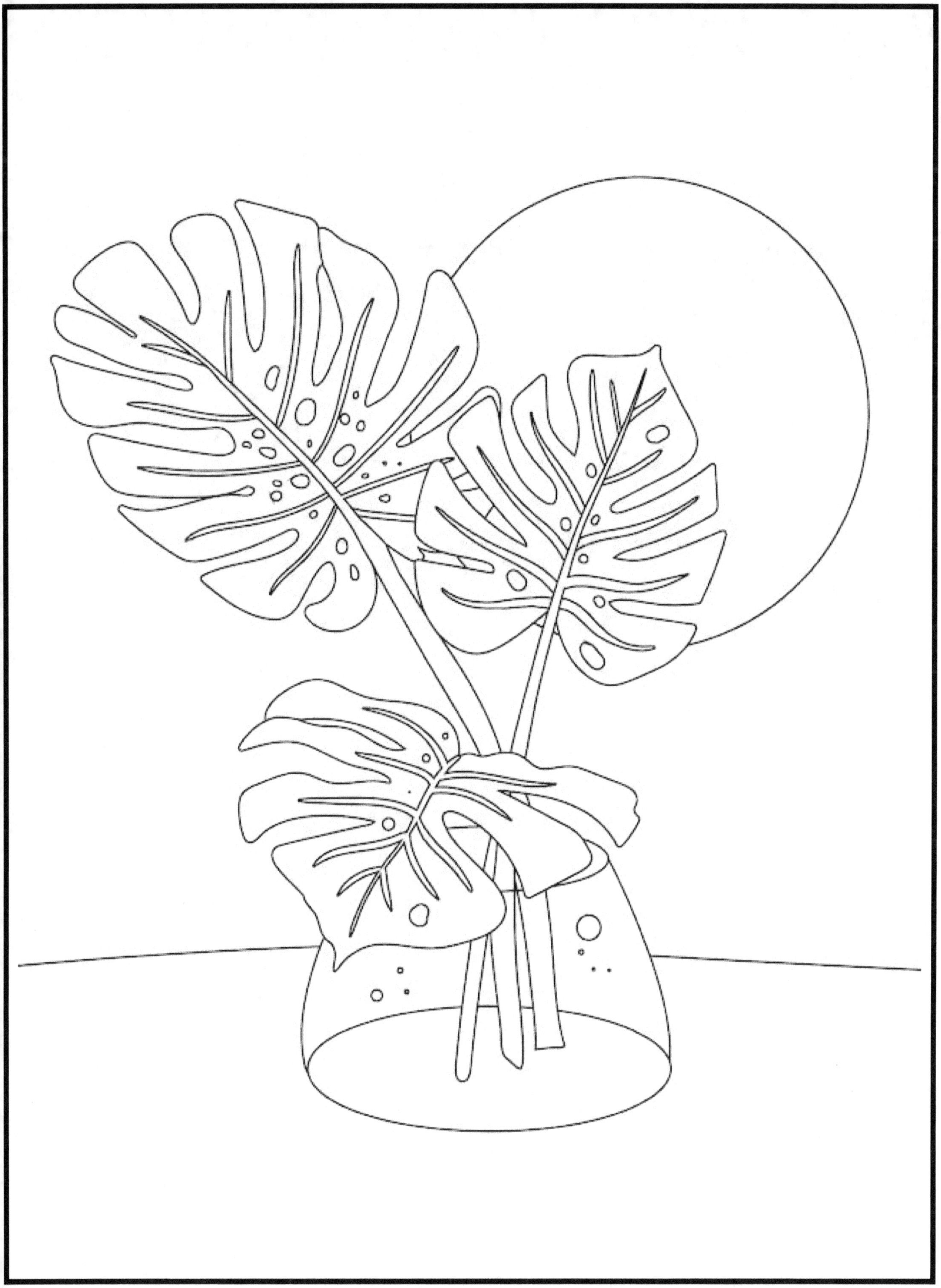

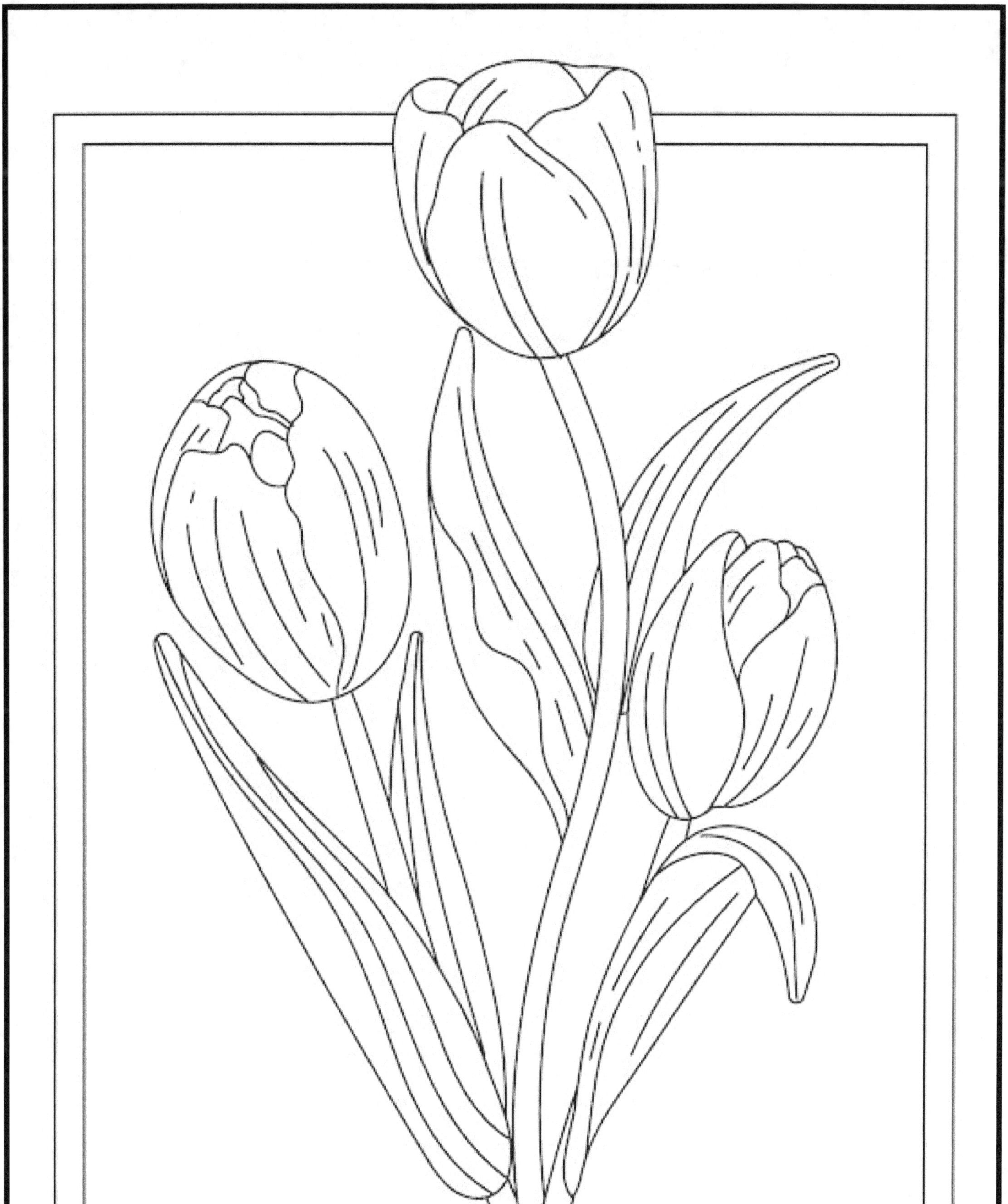

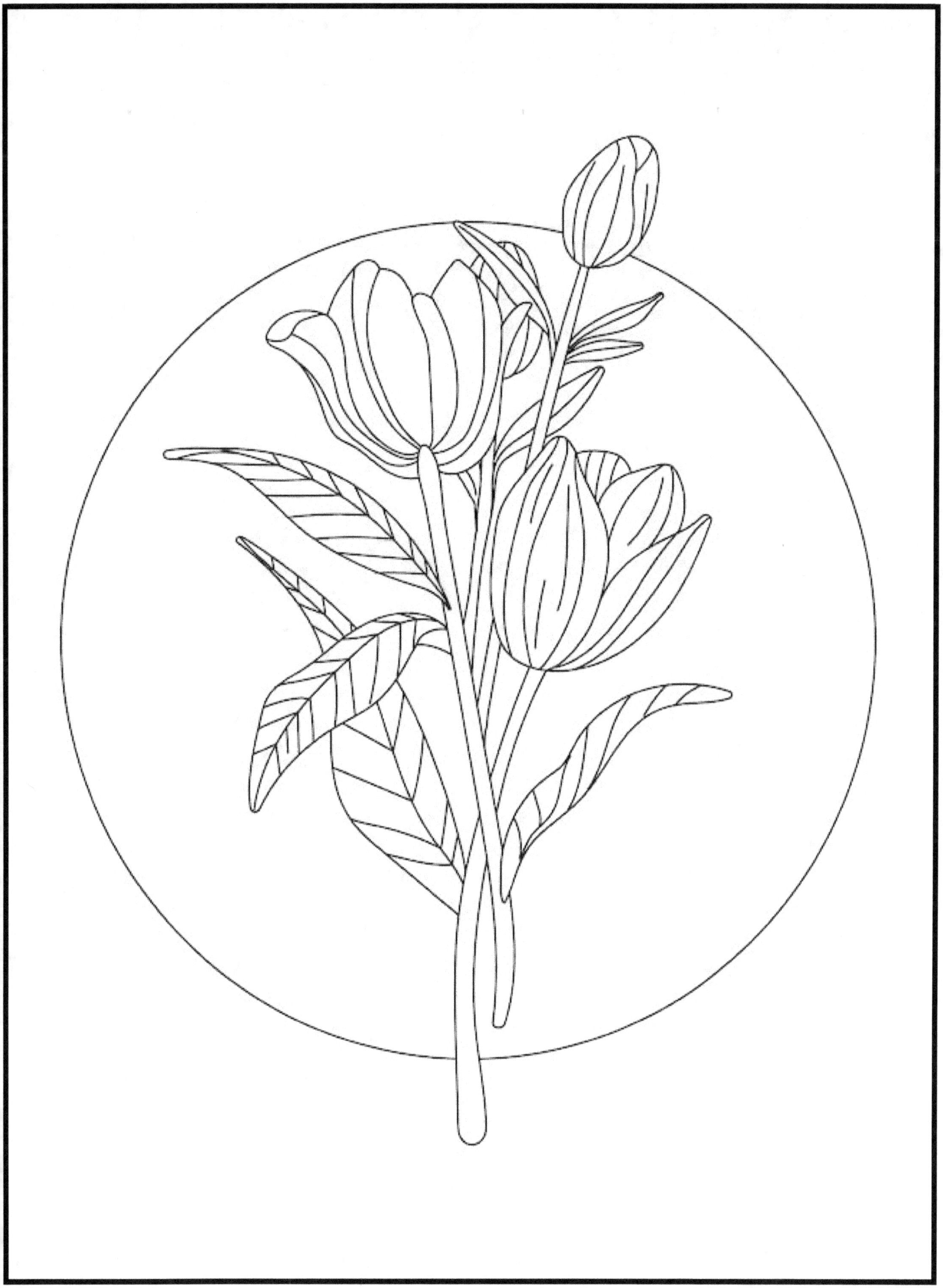

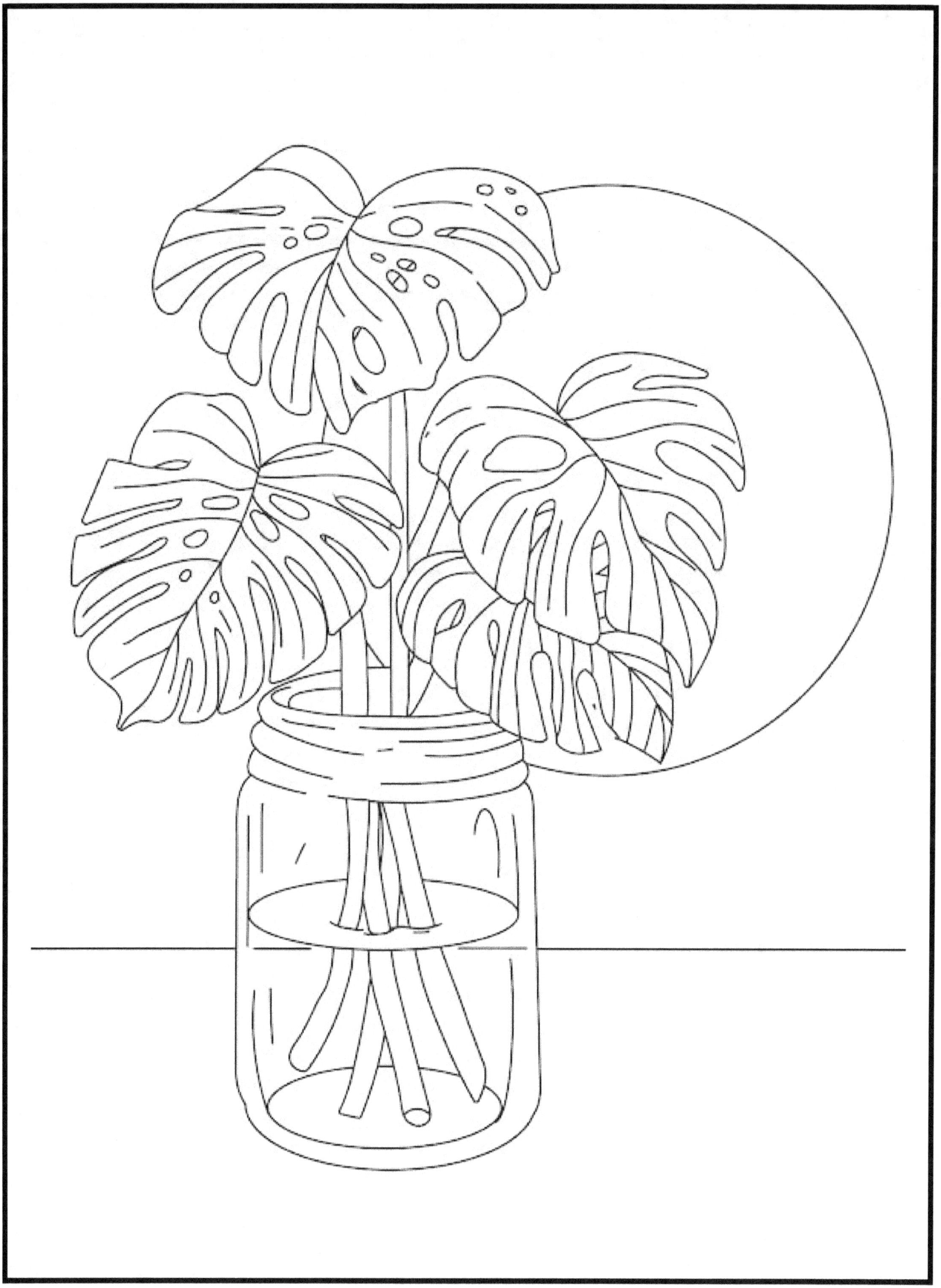

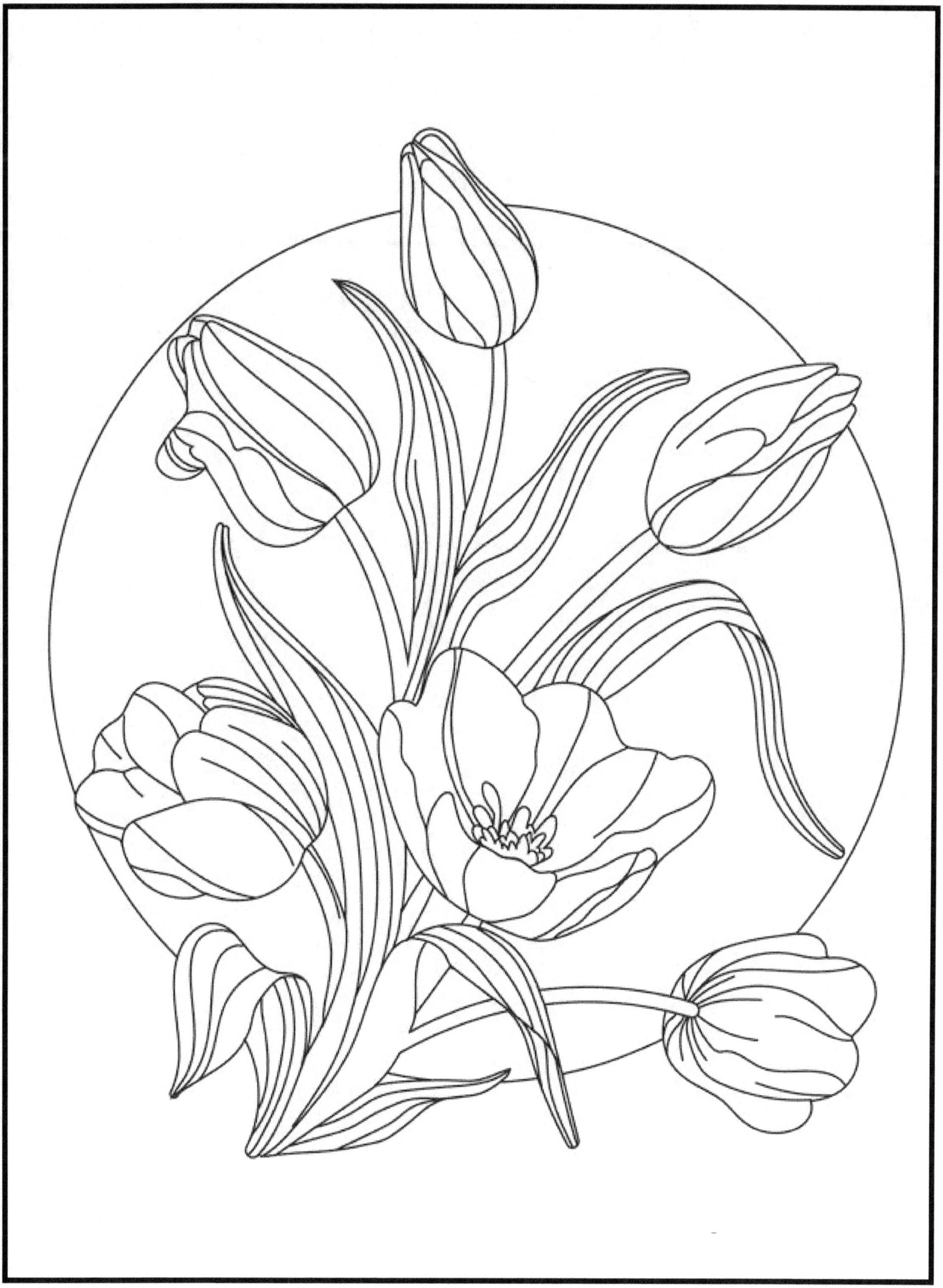

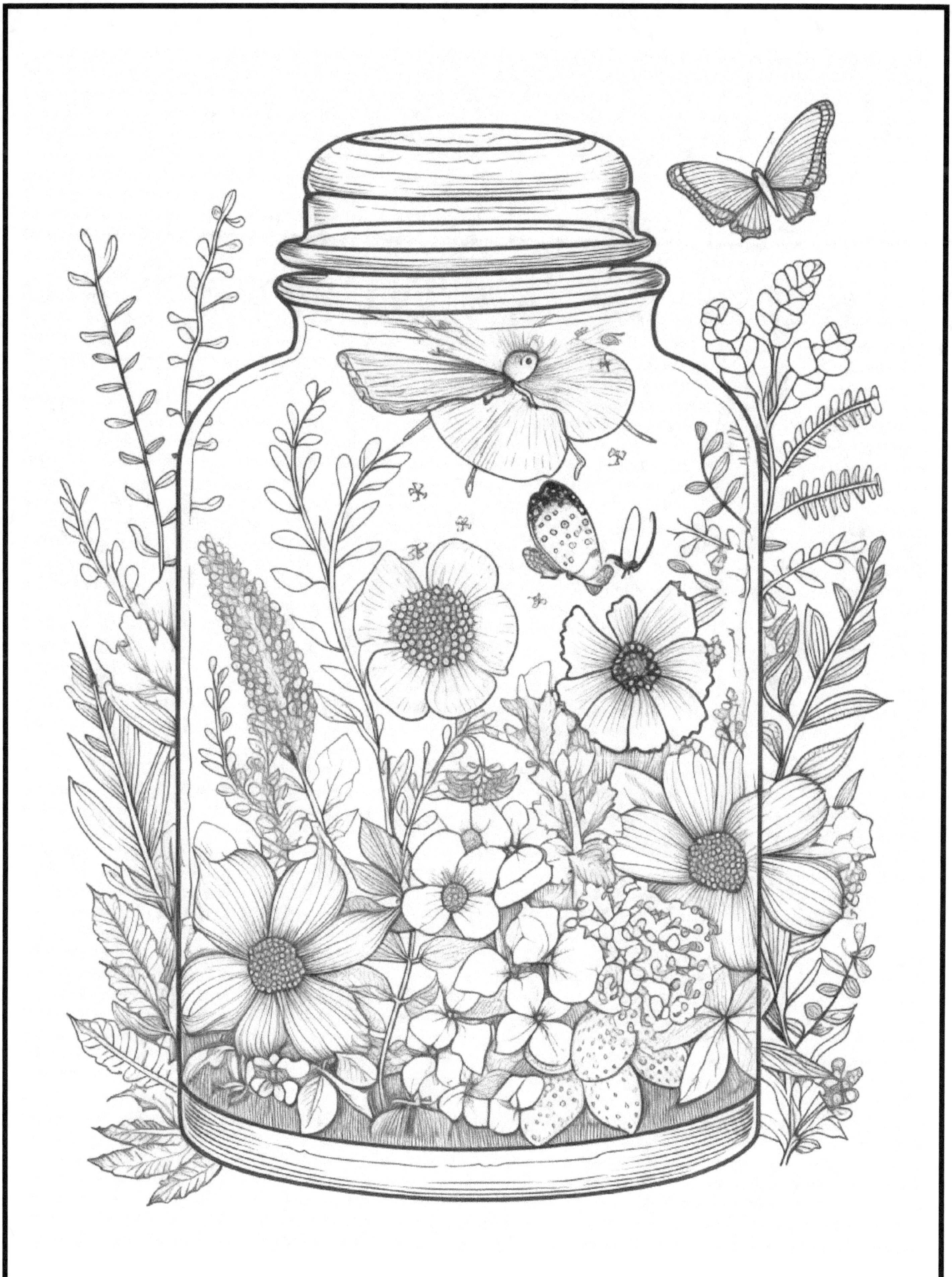

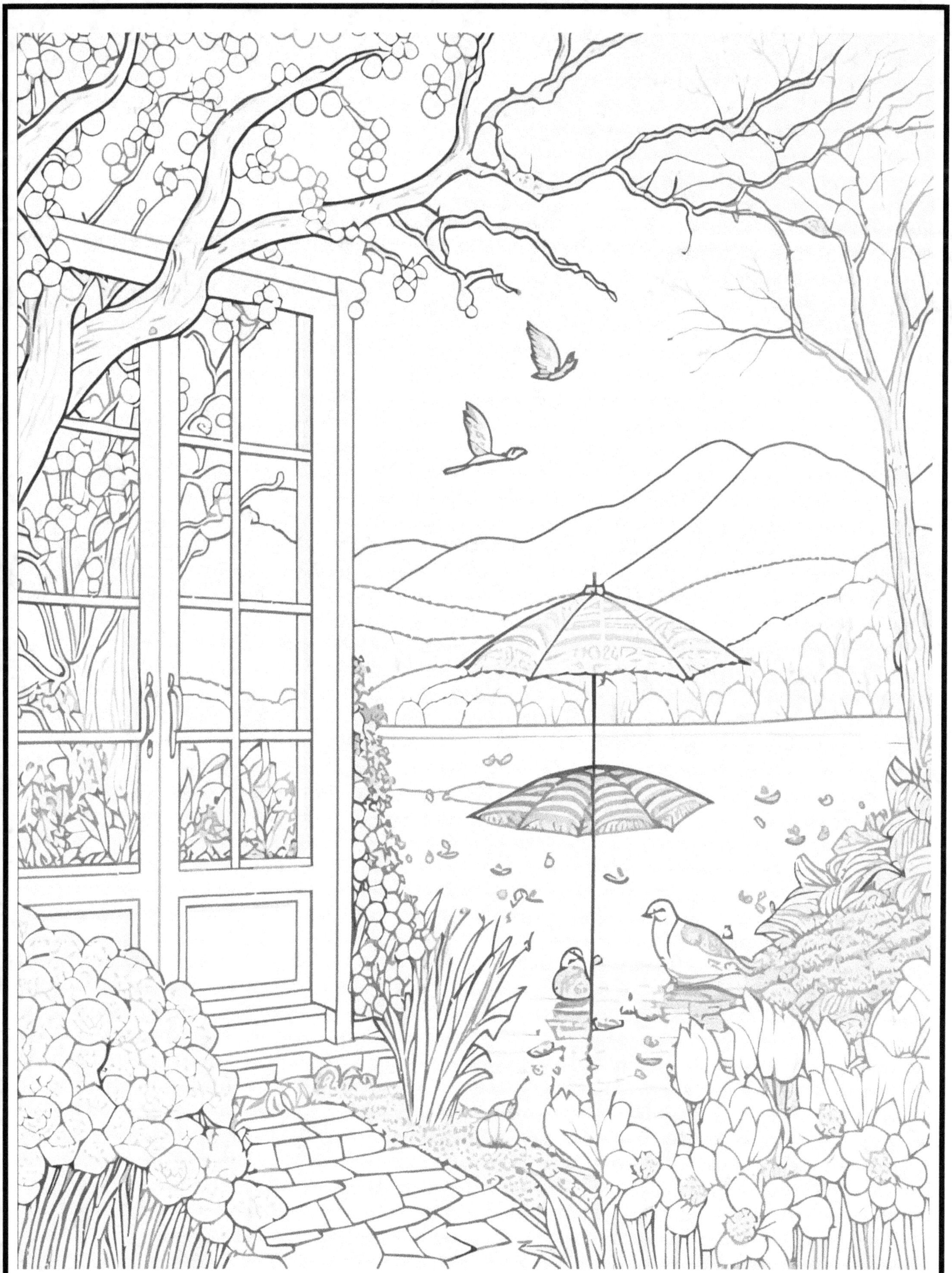

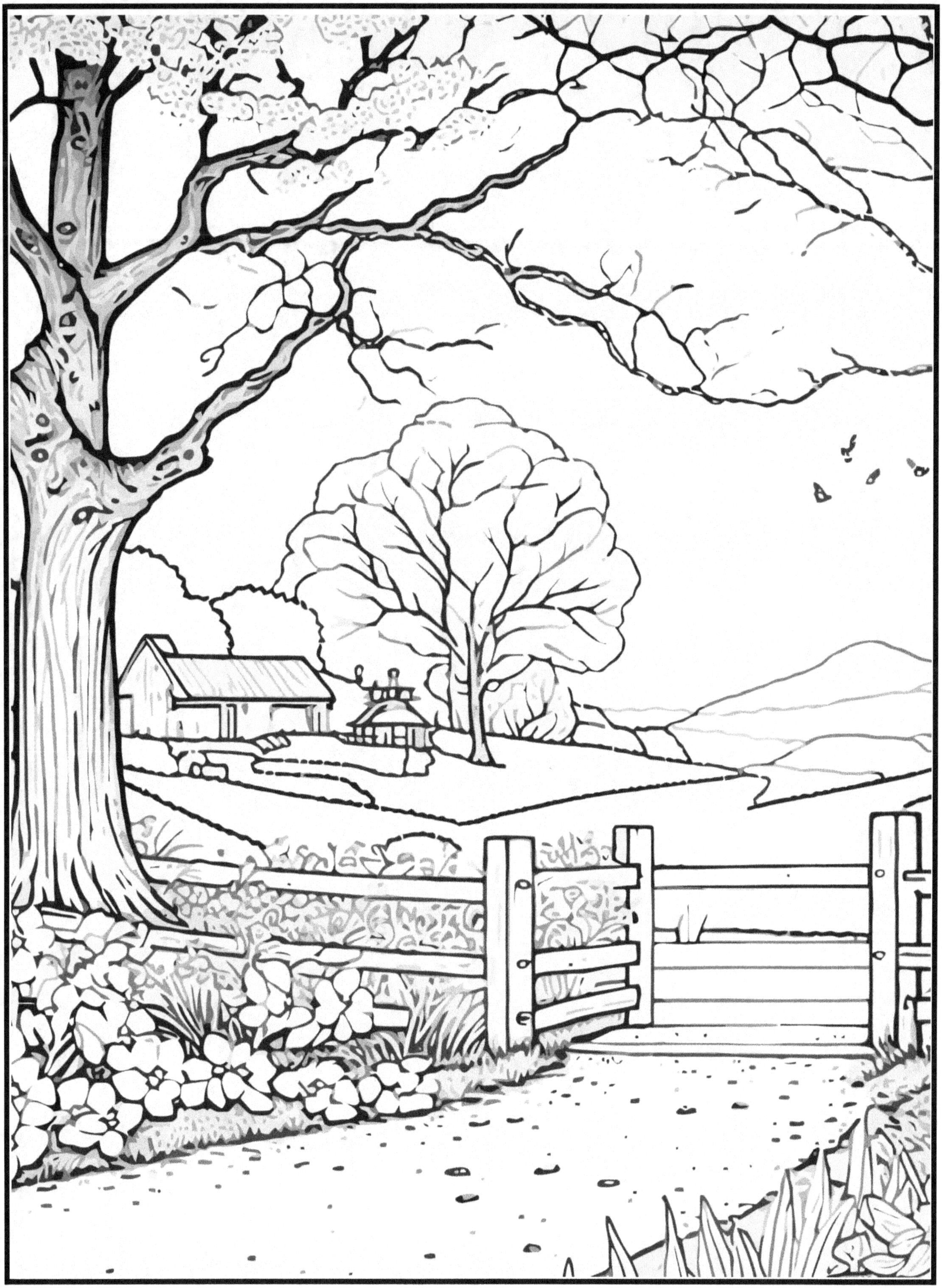

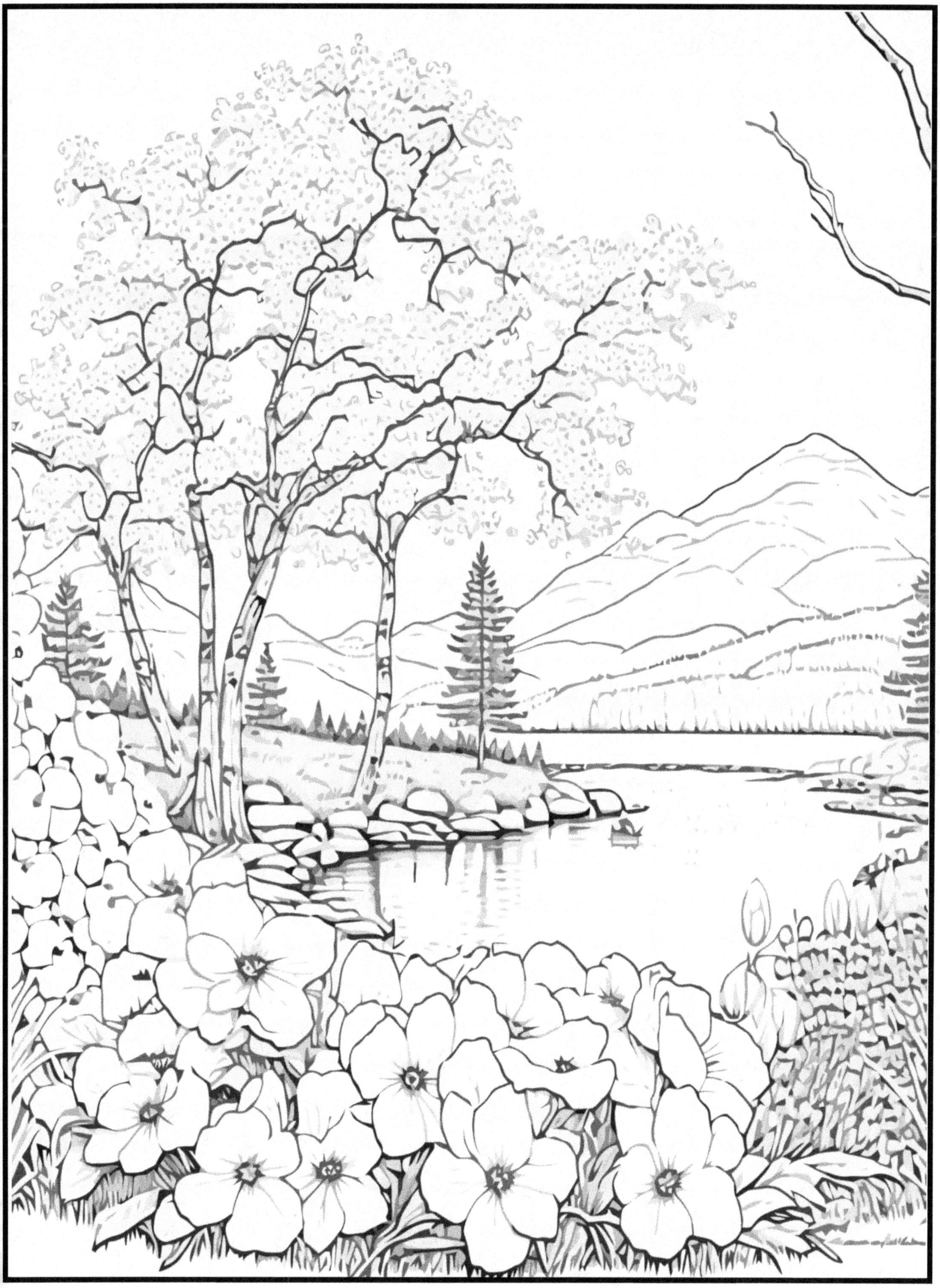

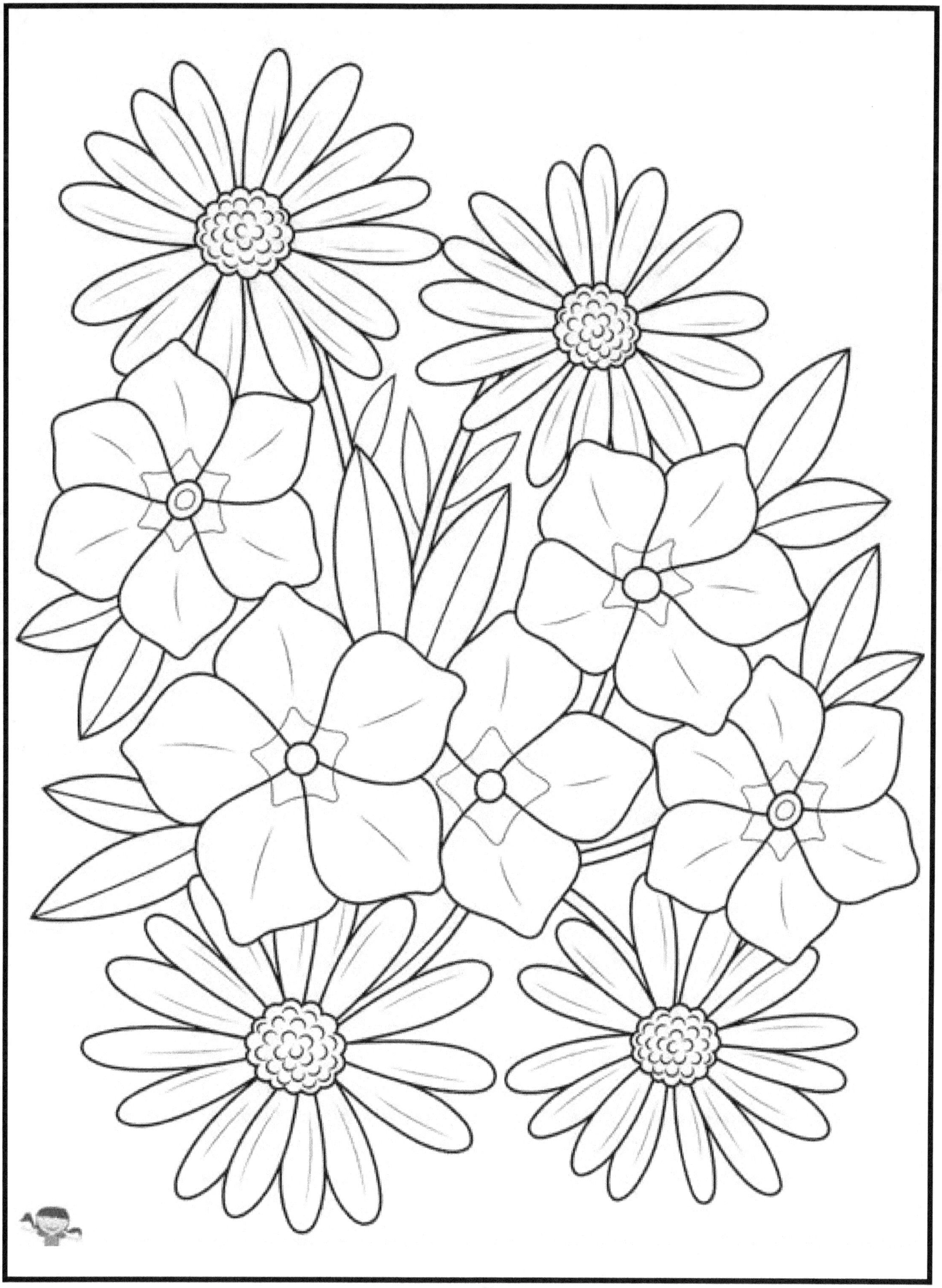

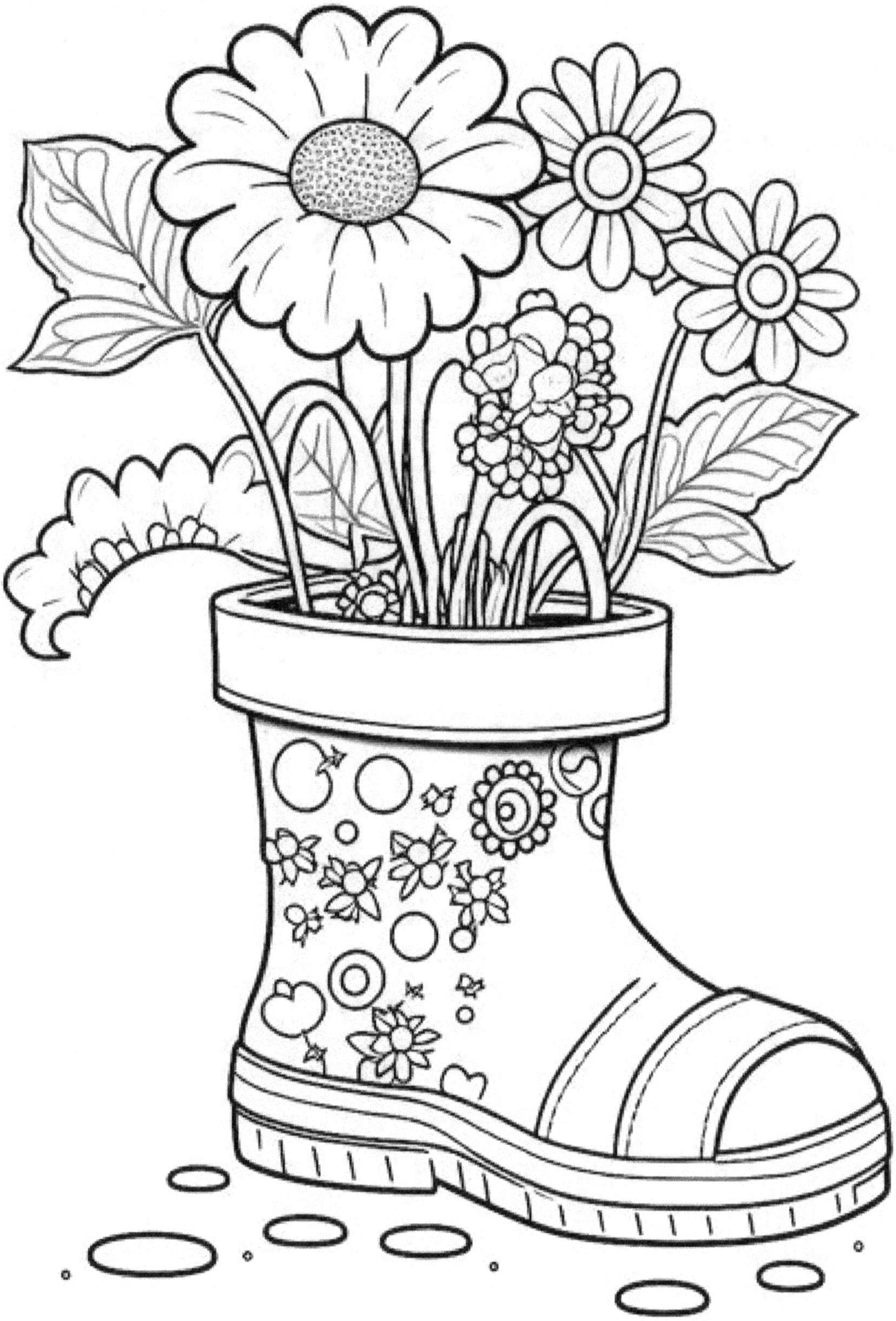

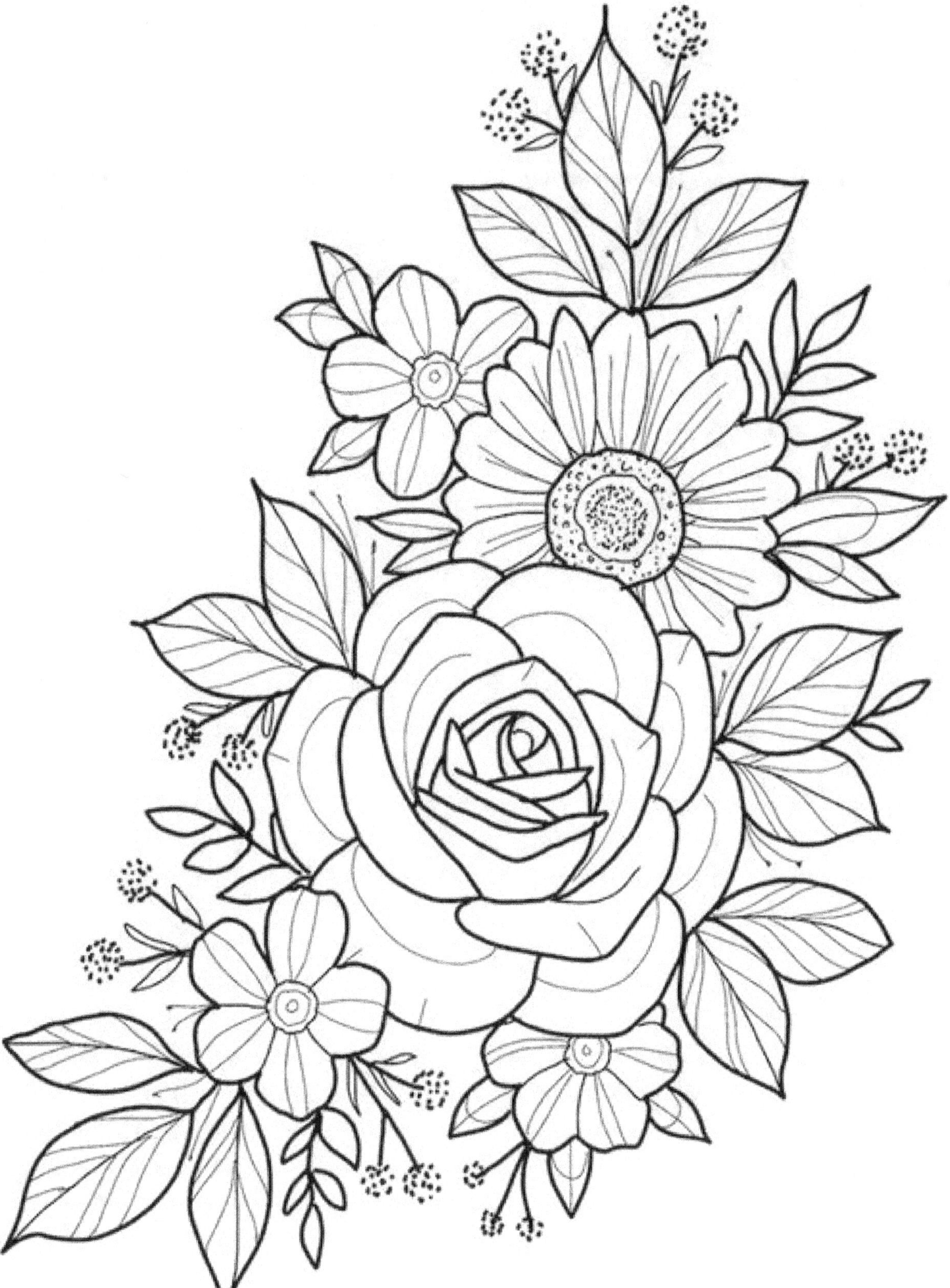

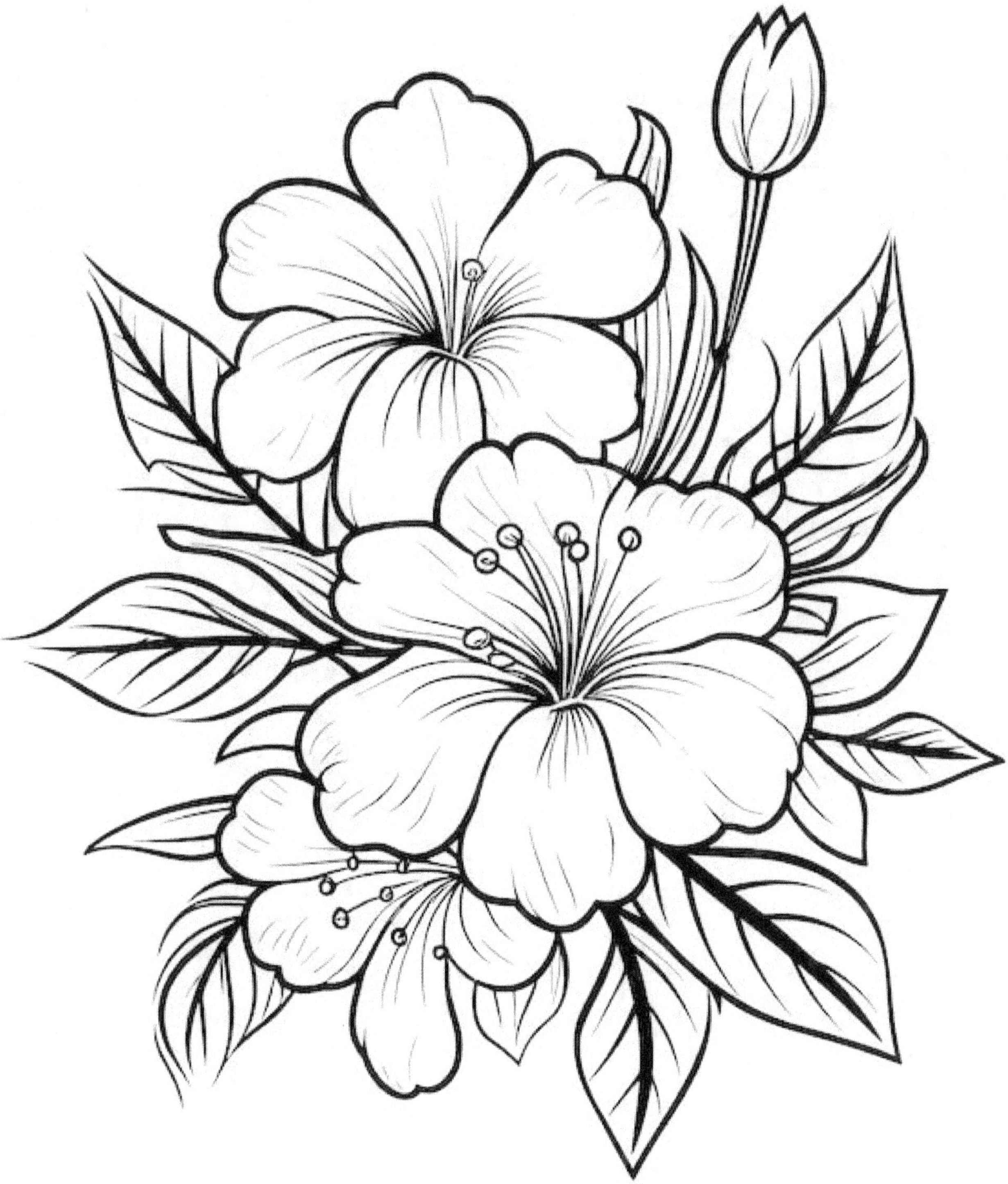

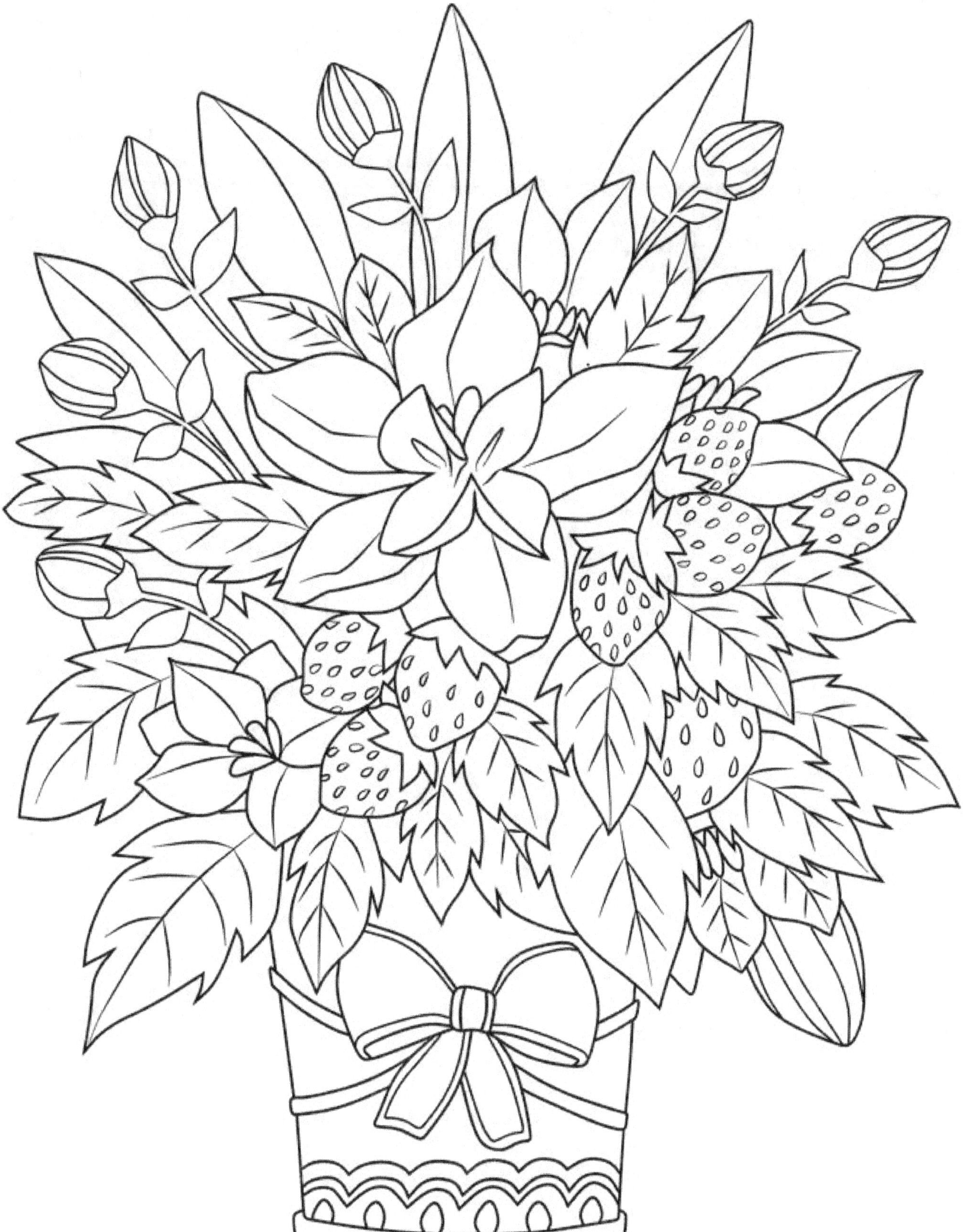

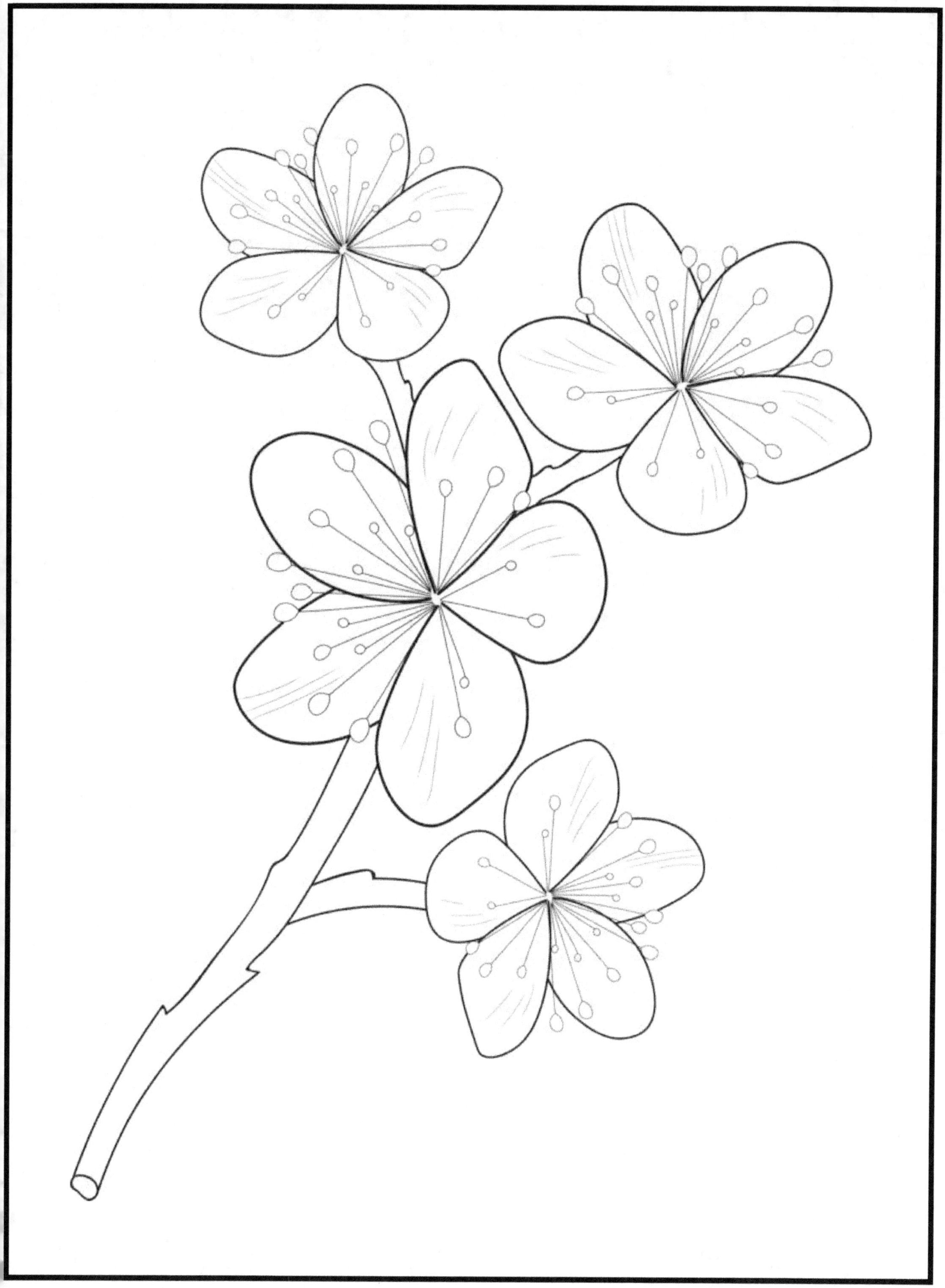

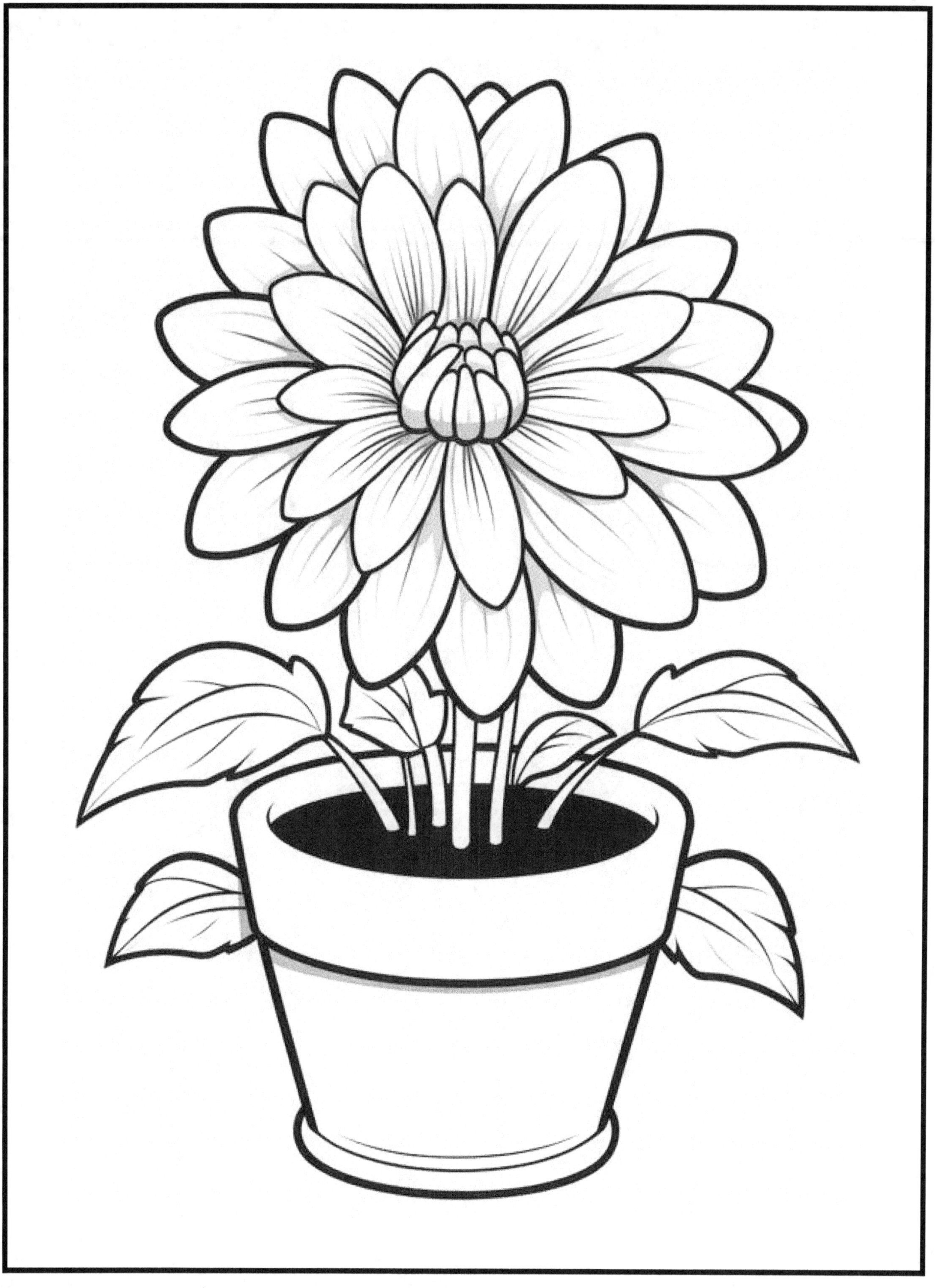

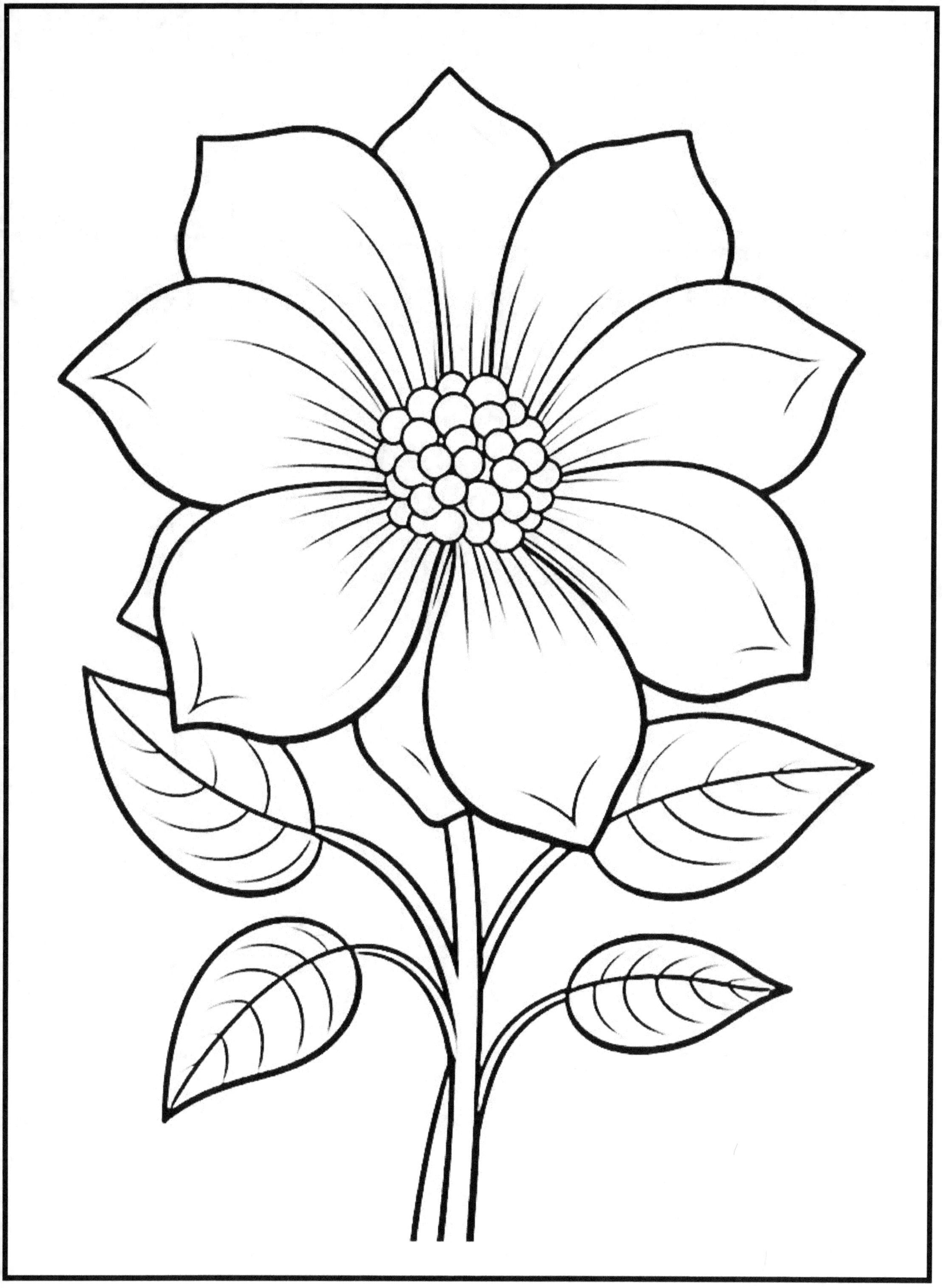

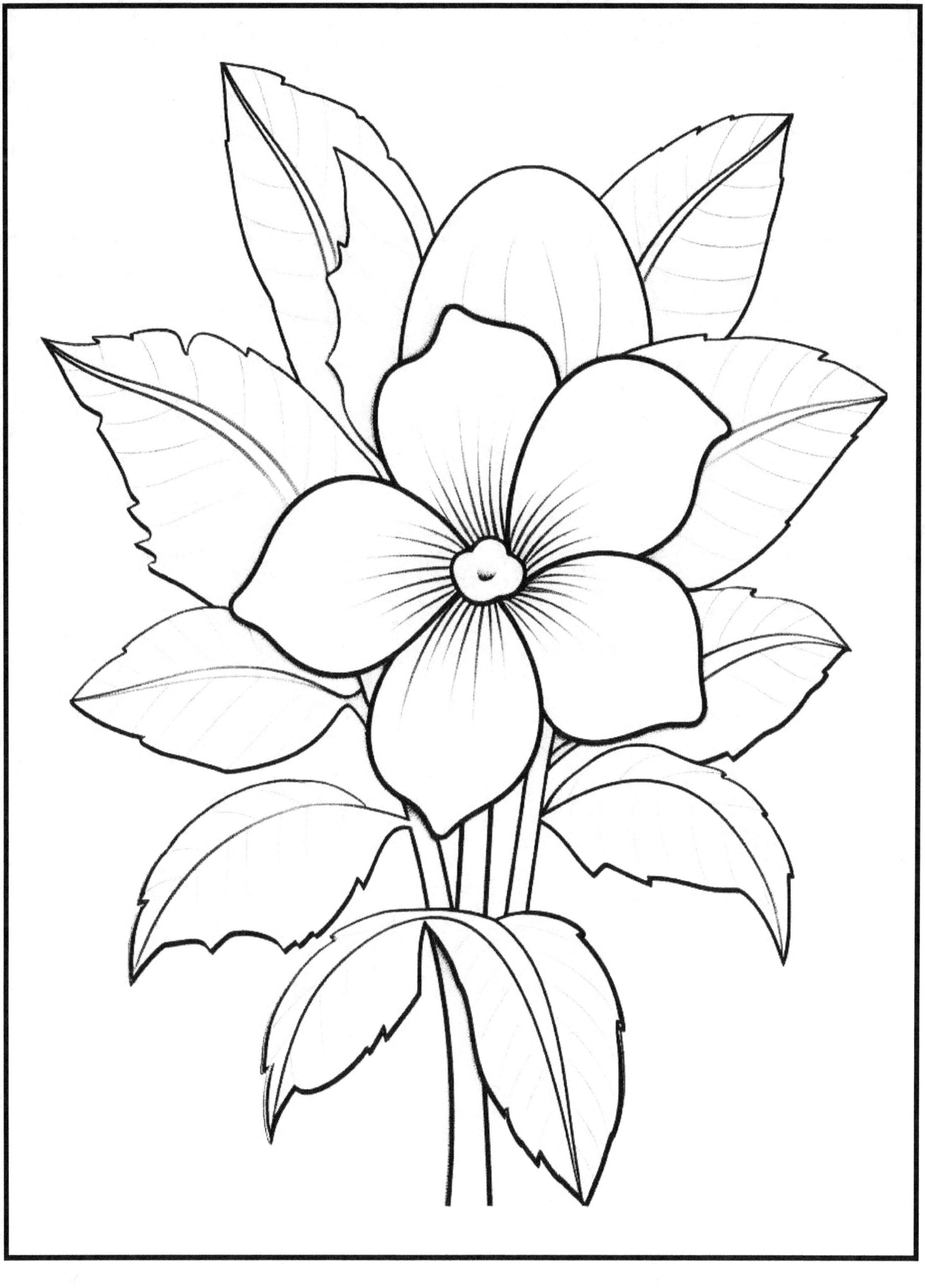

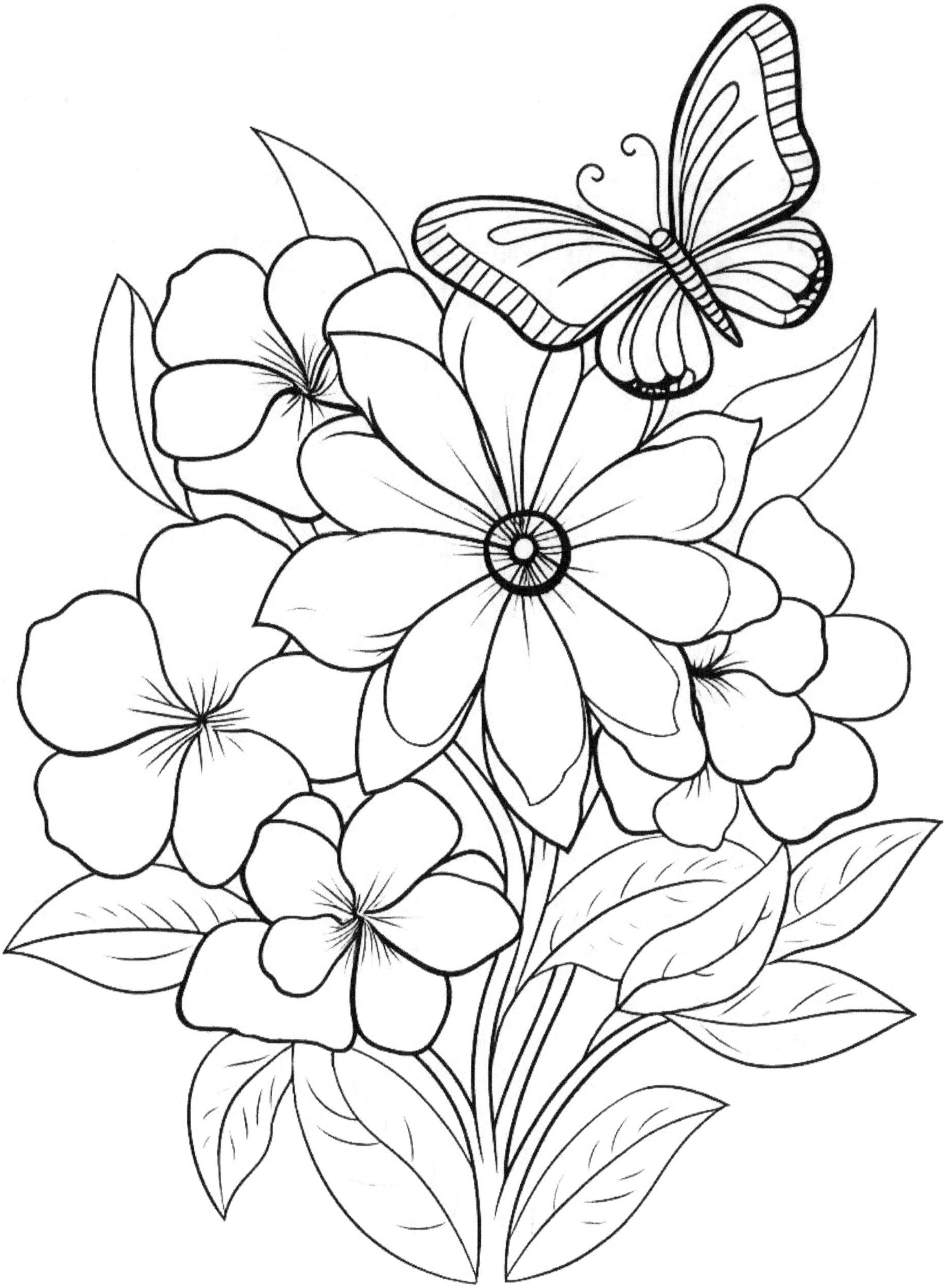

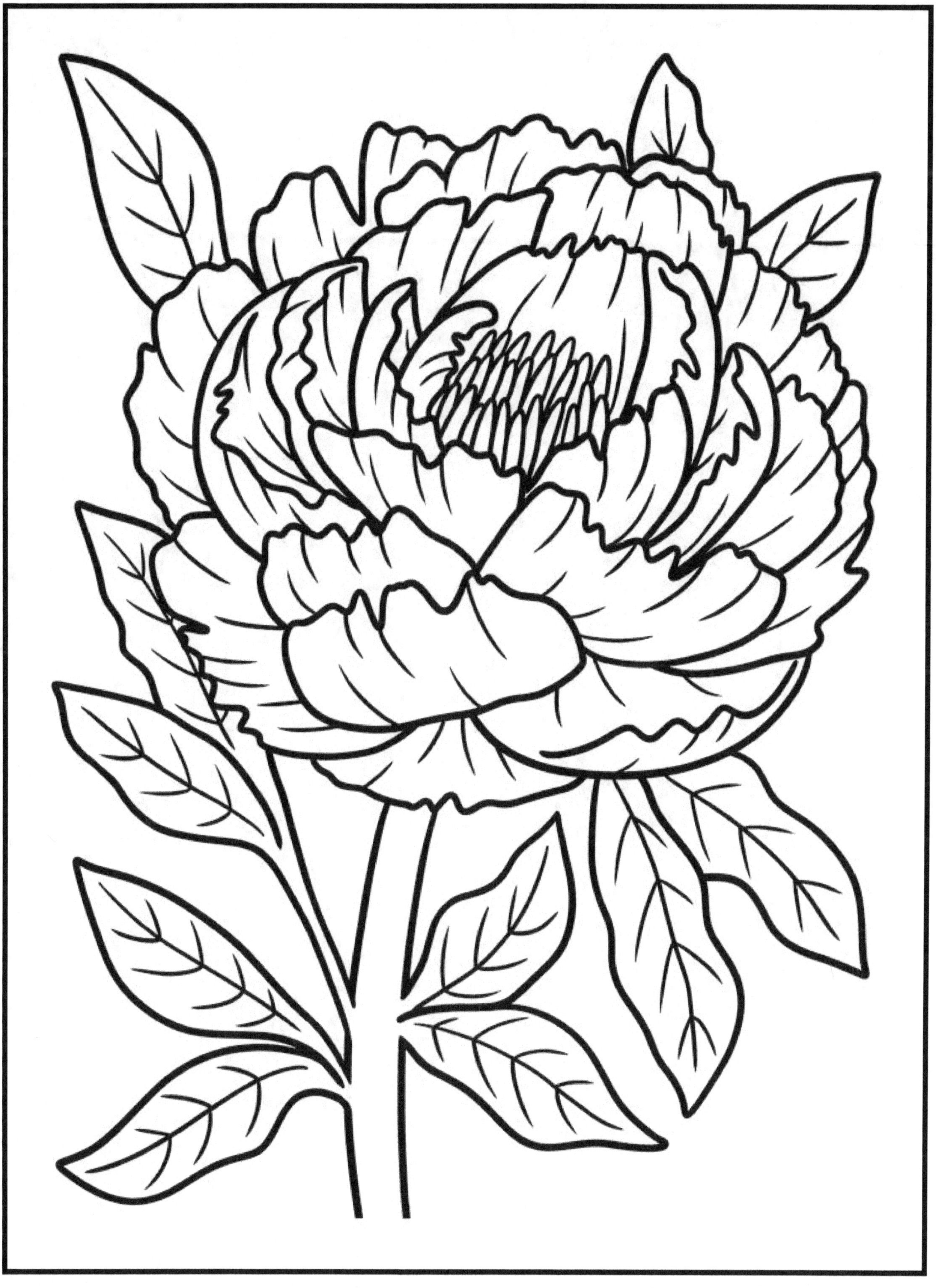

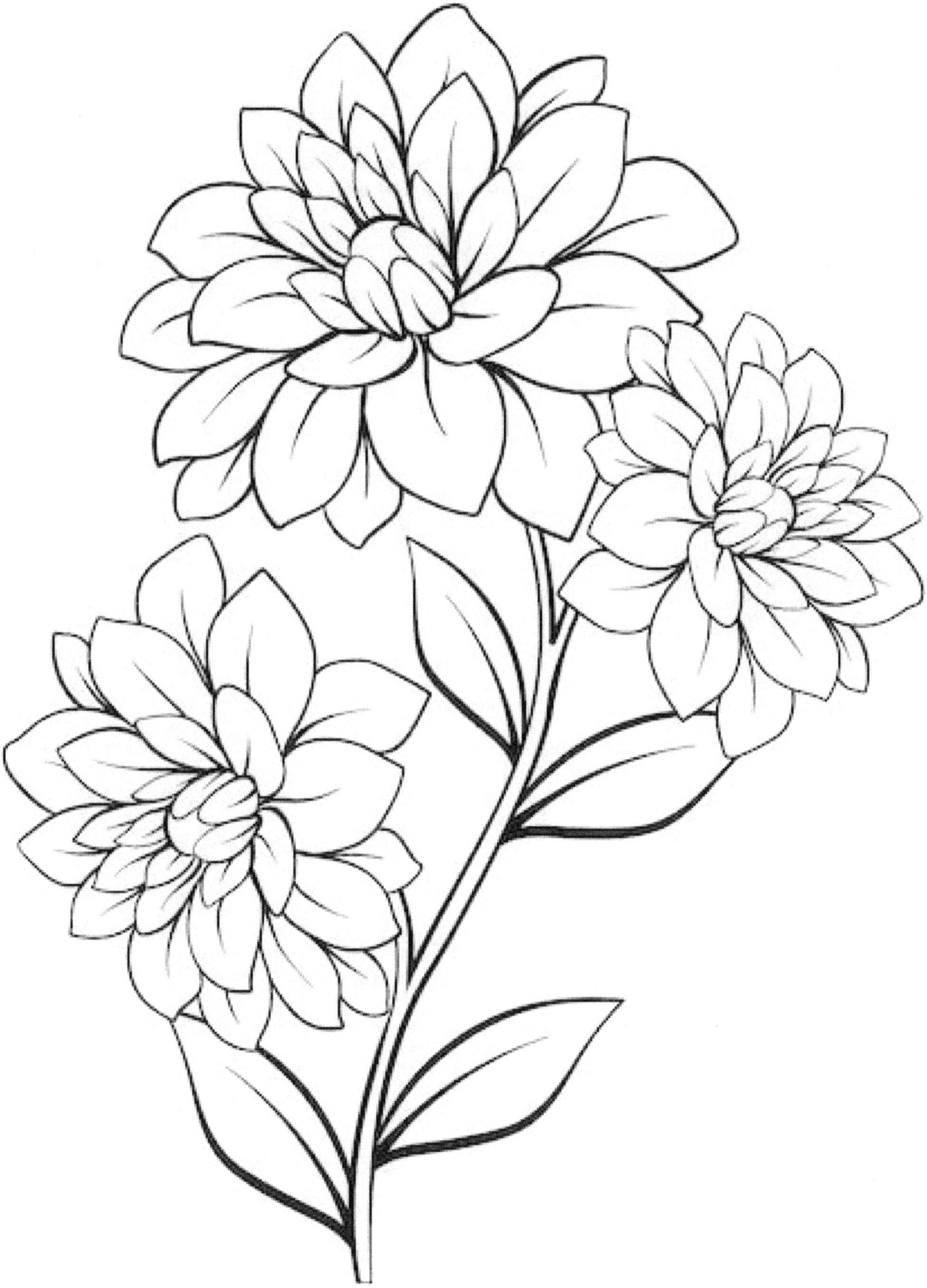

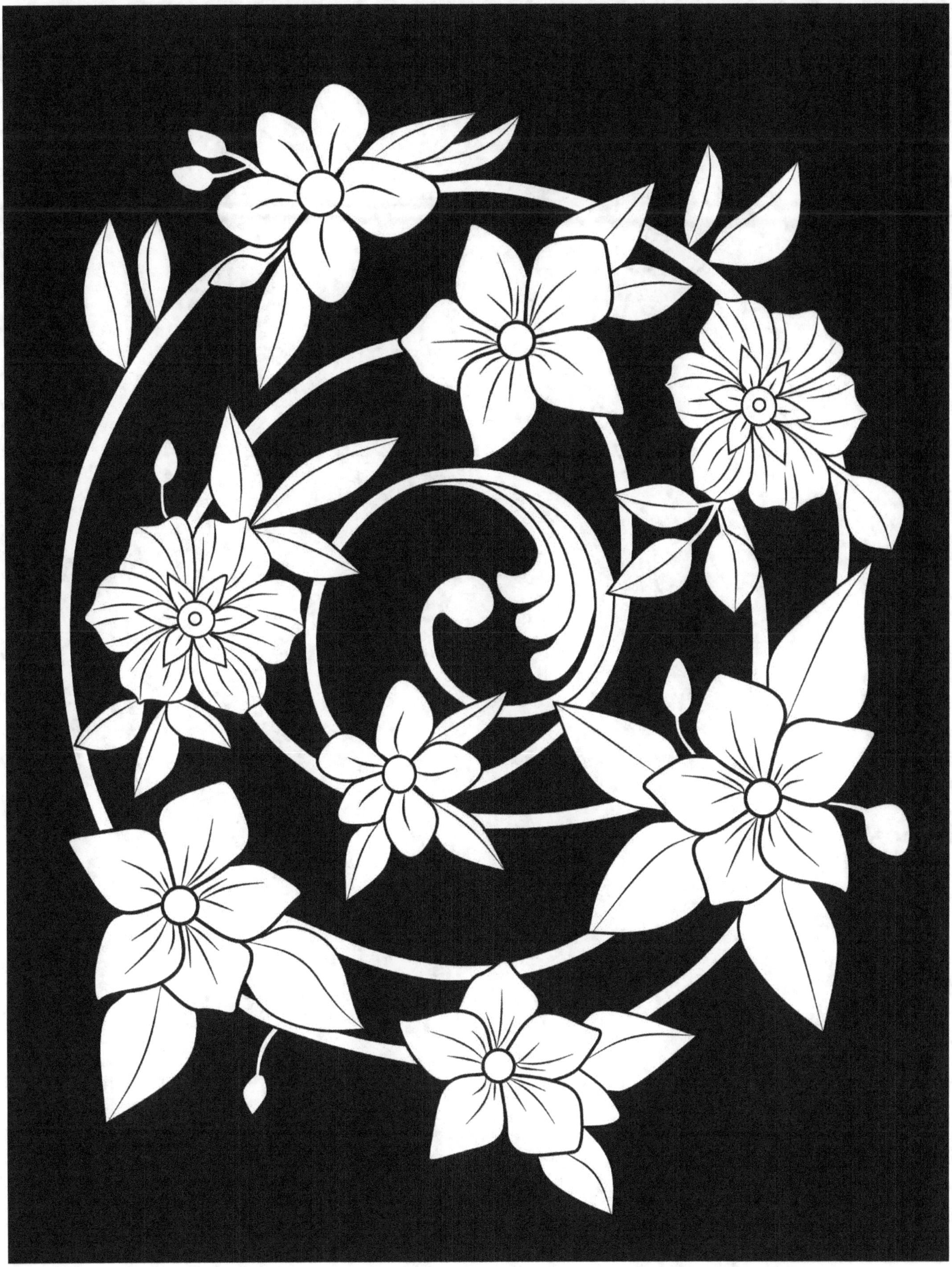

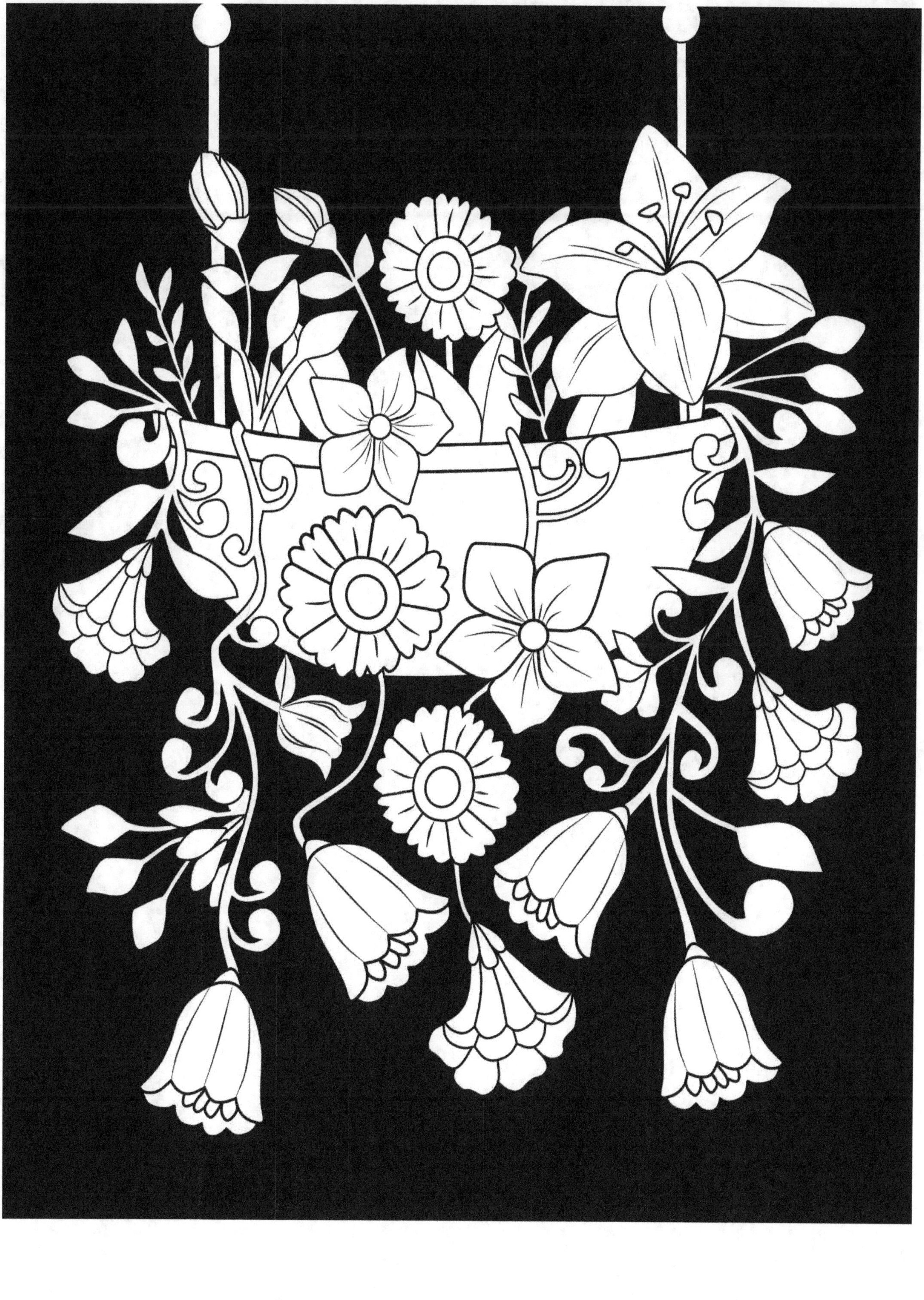

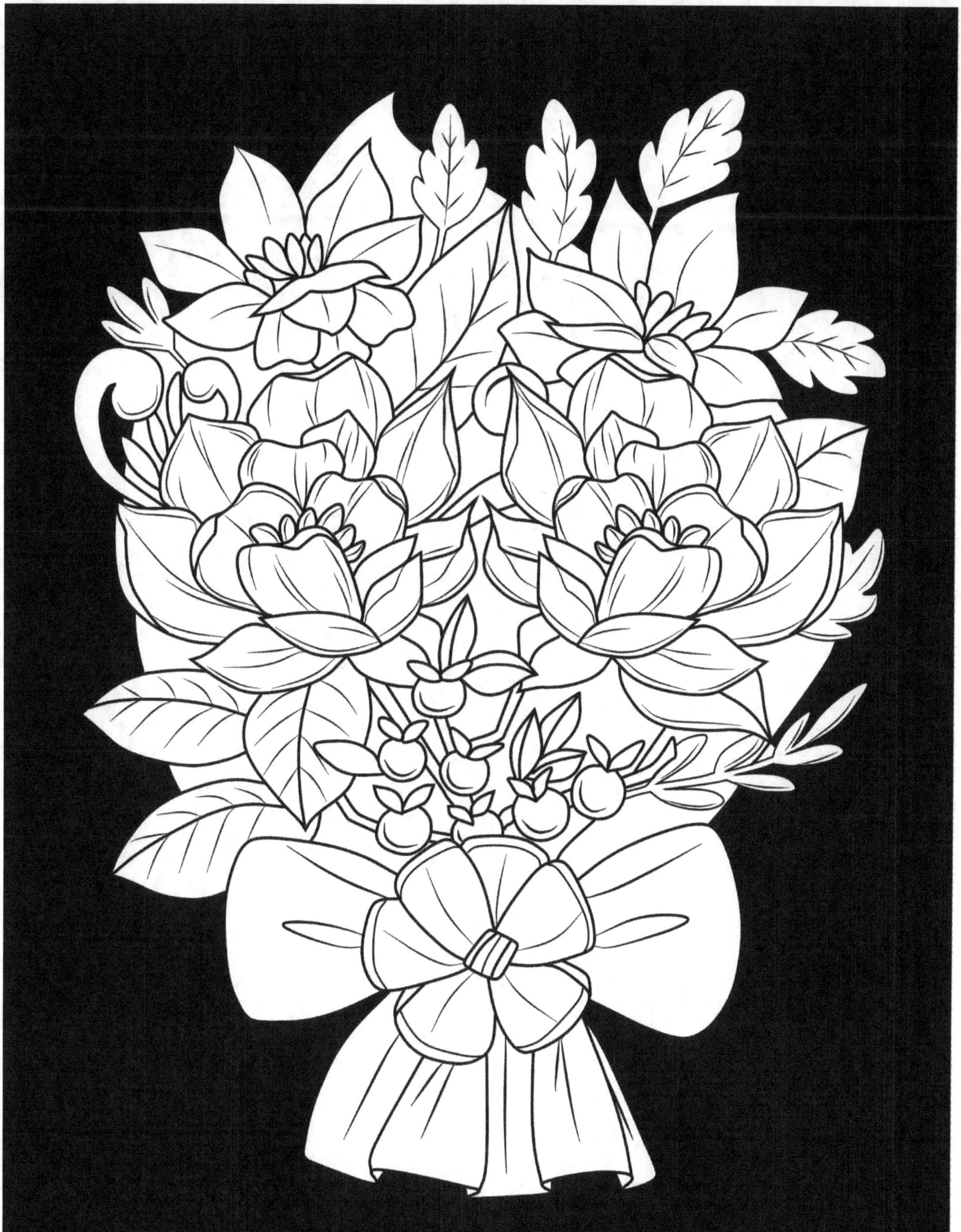

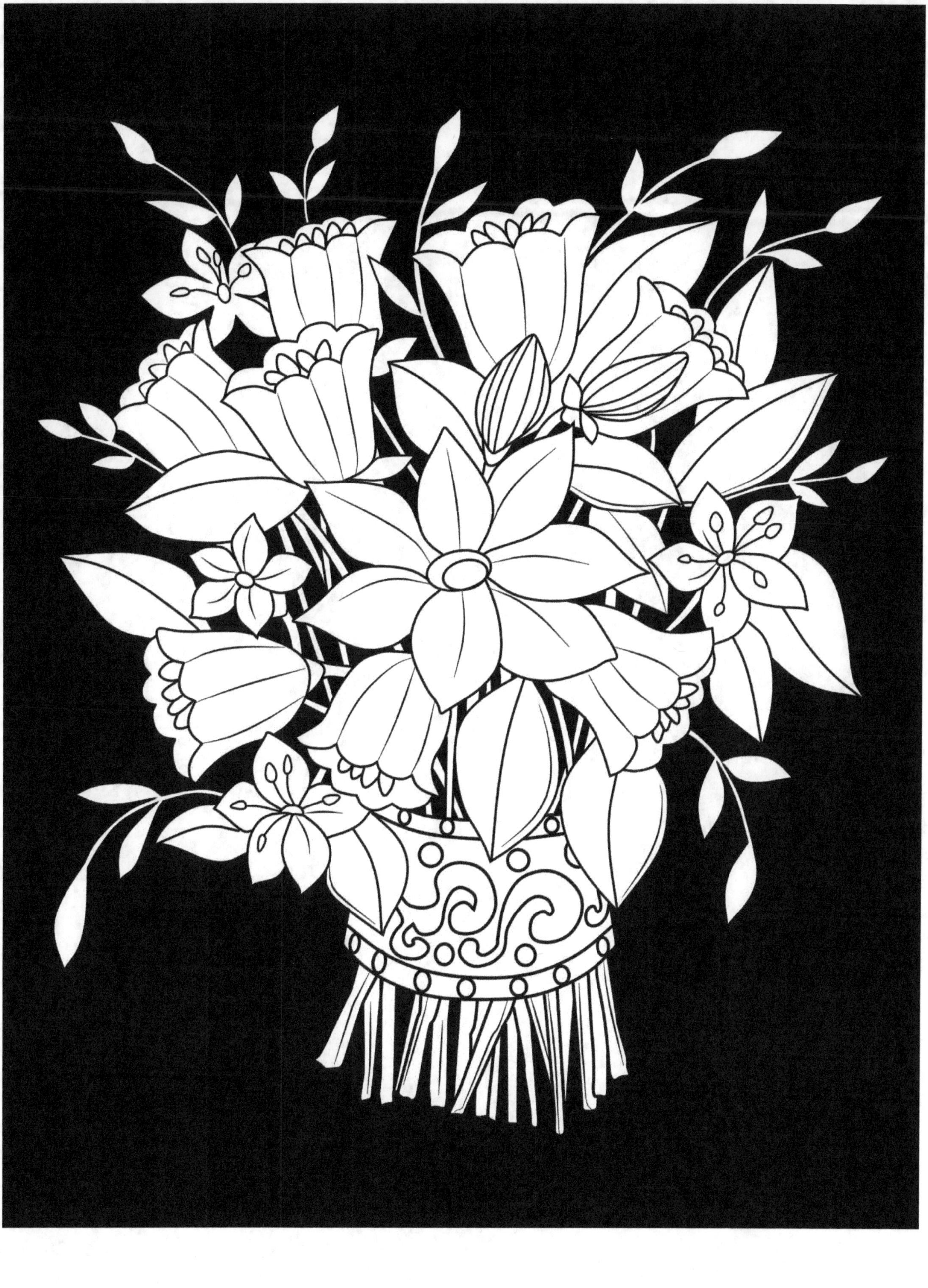

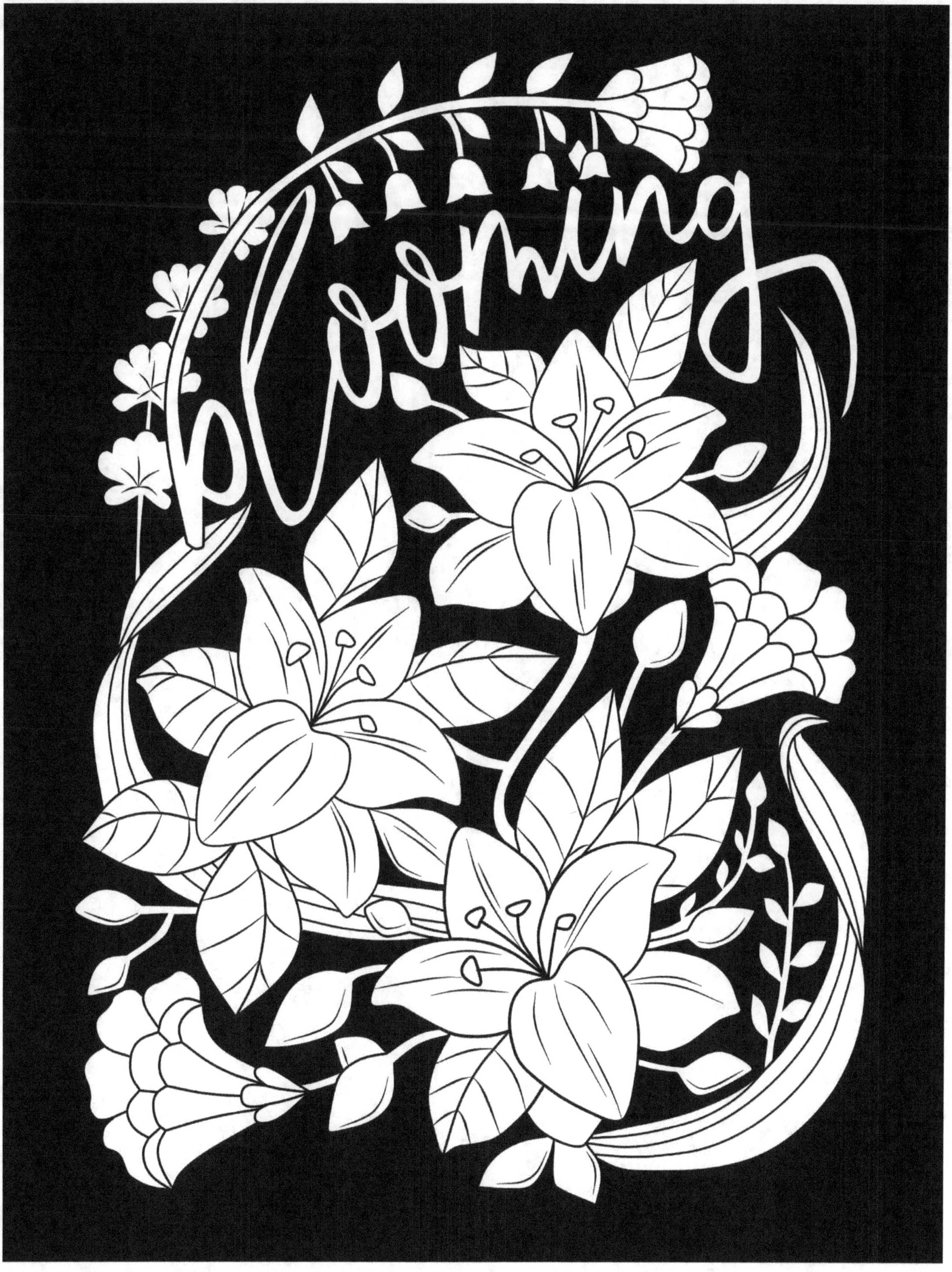
blooming

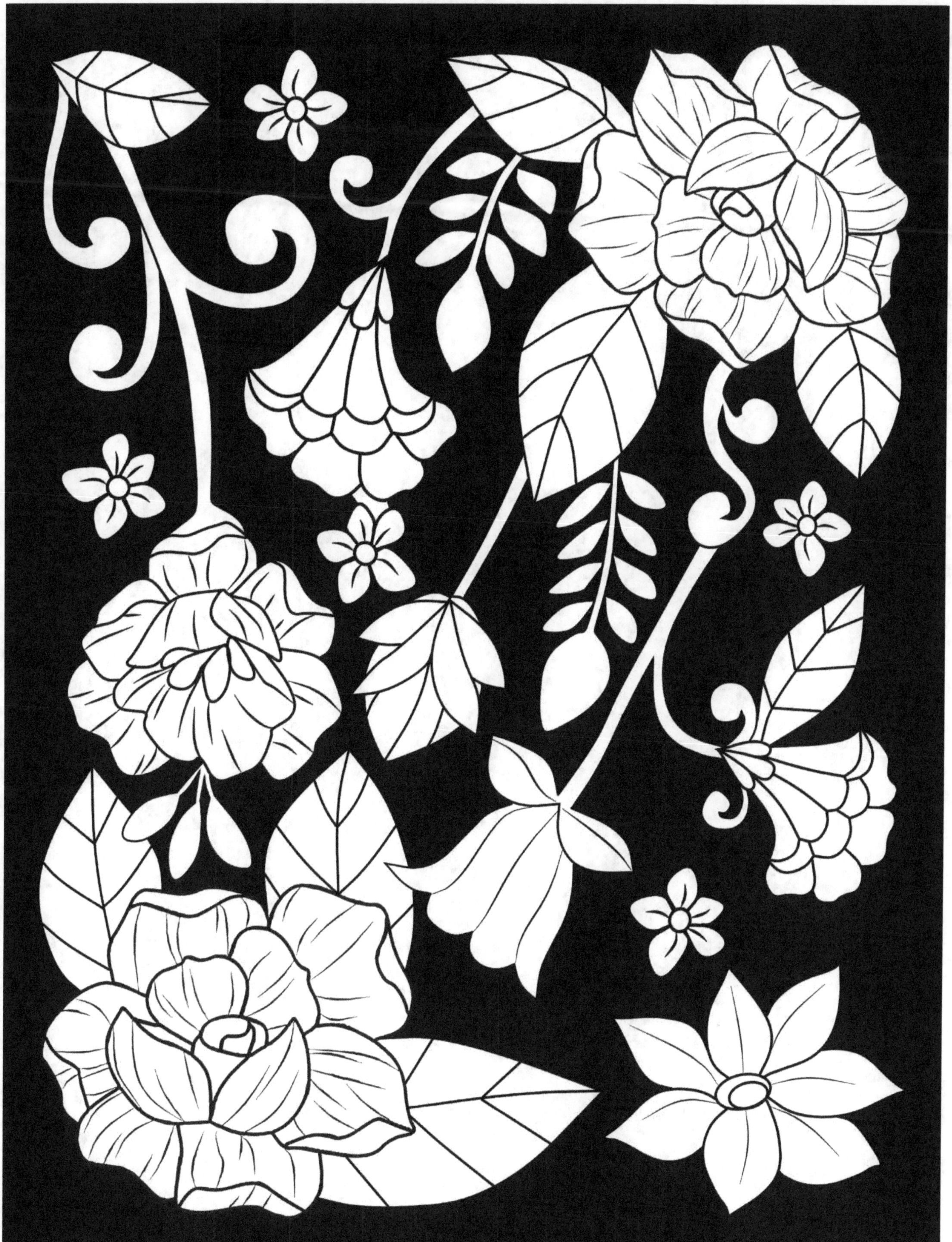

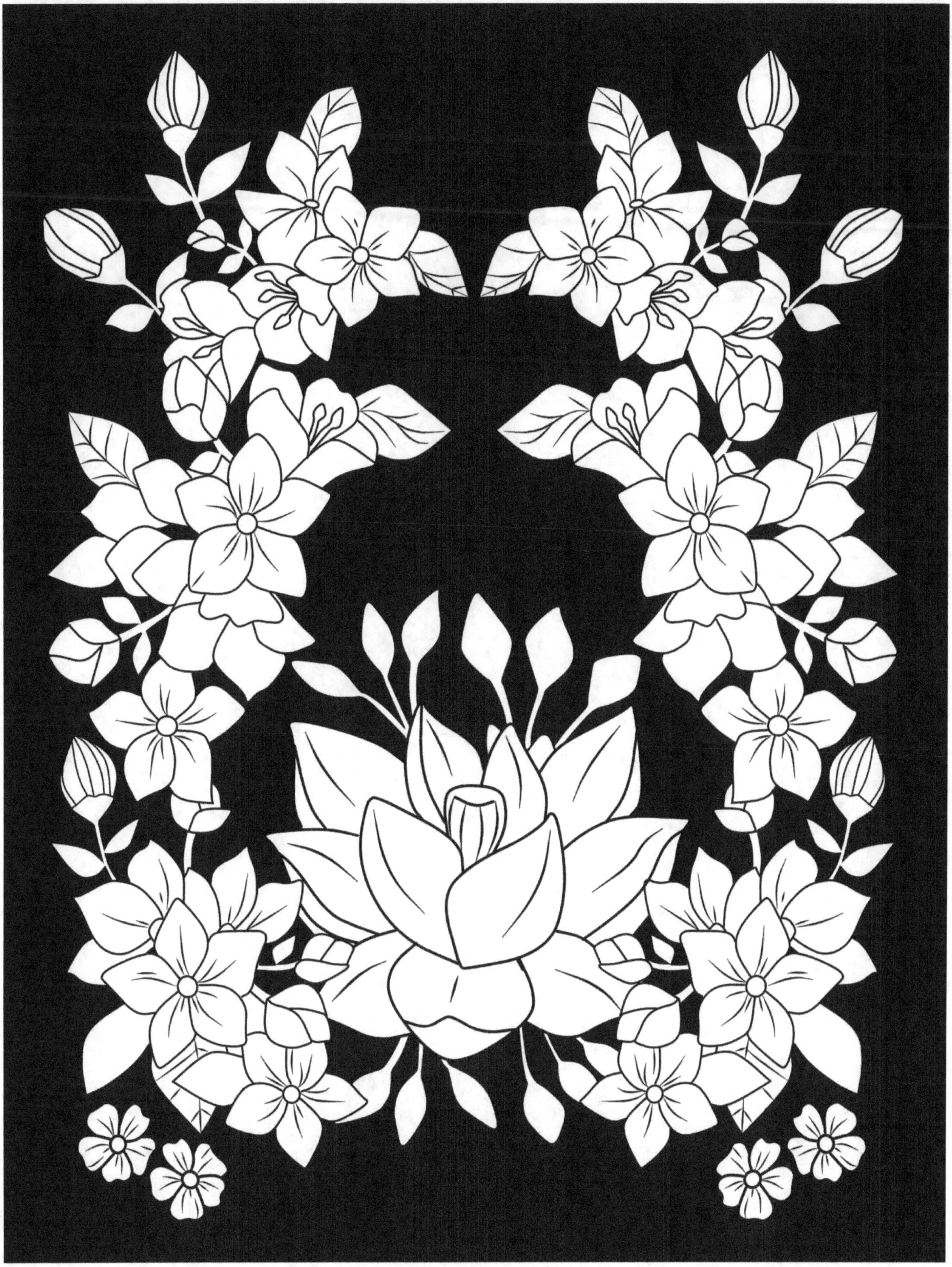

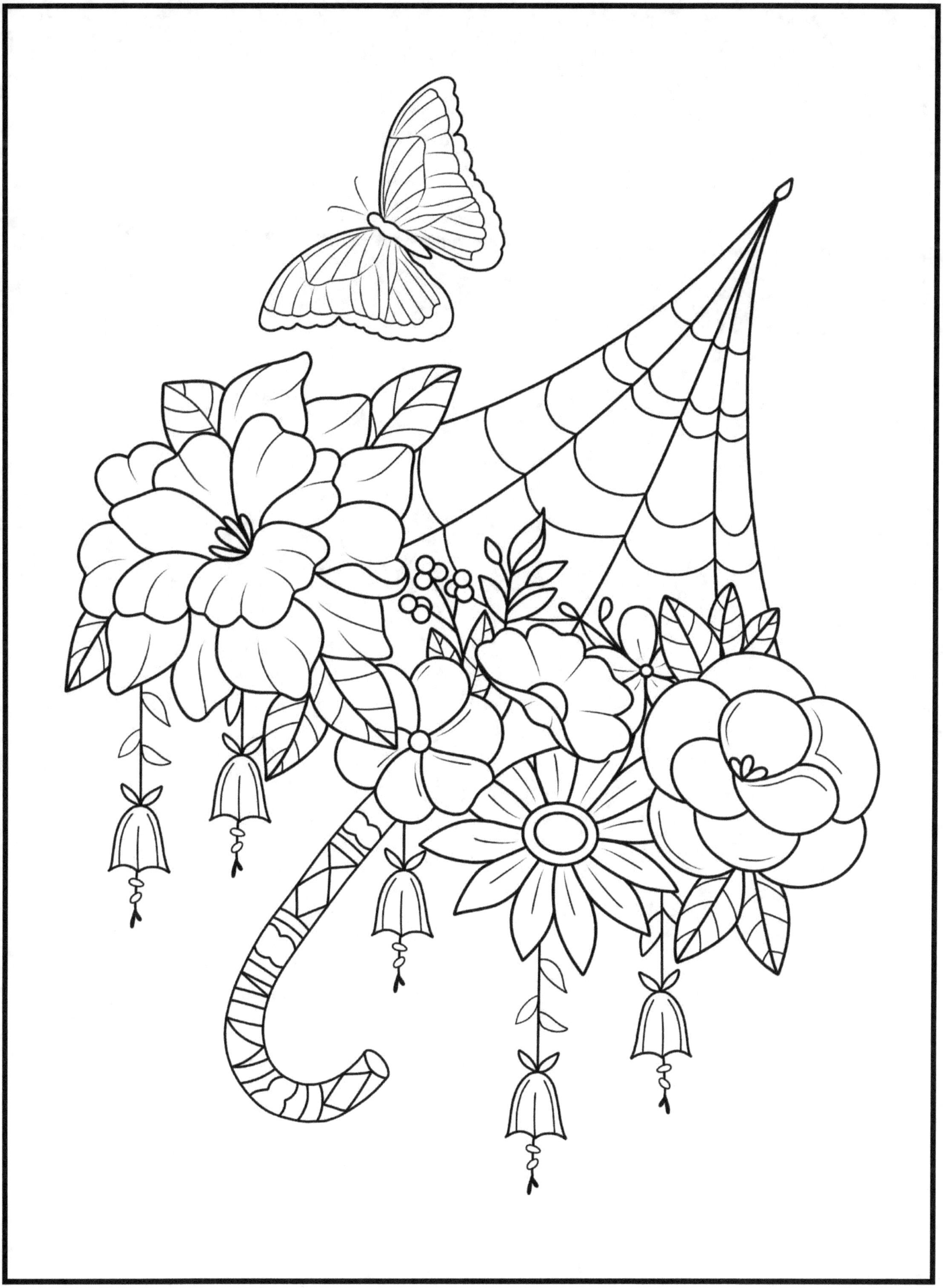

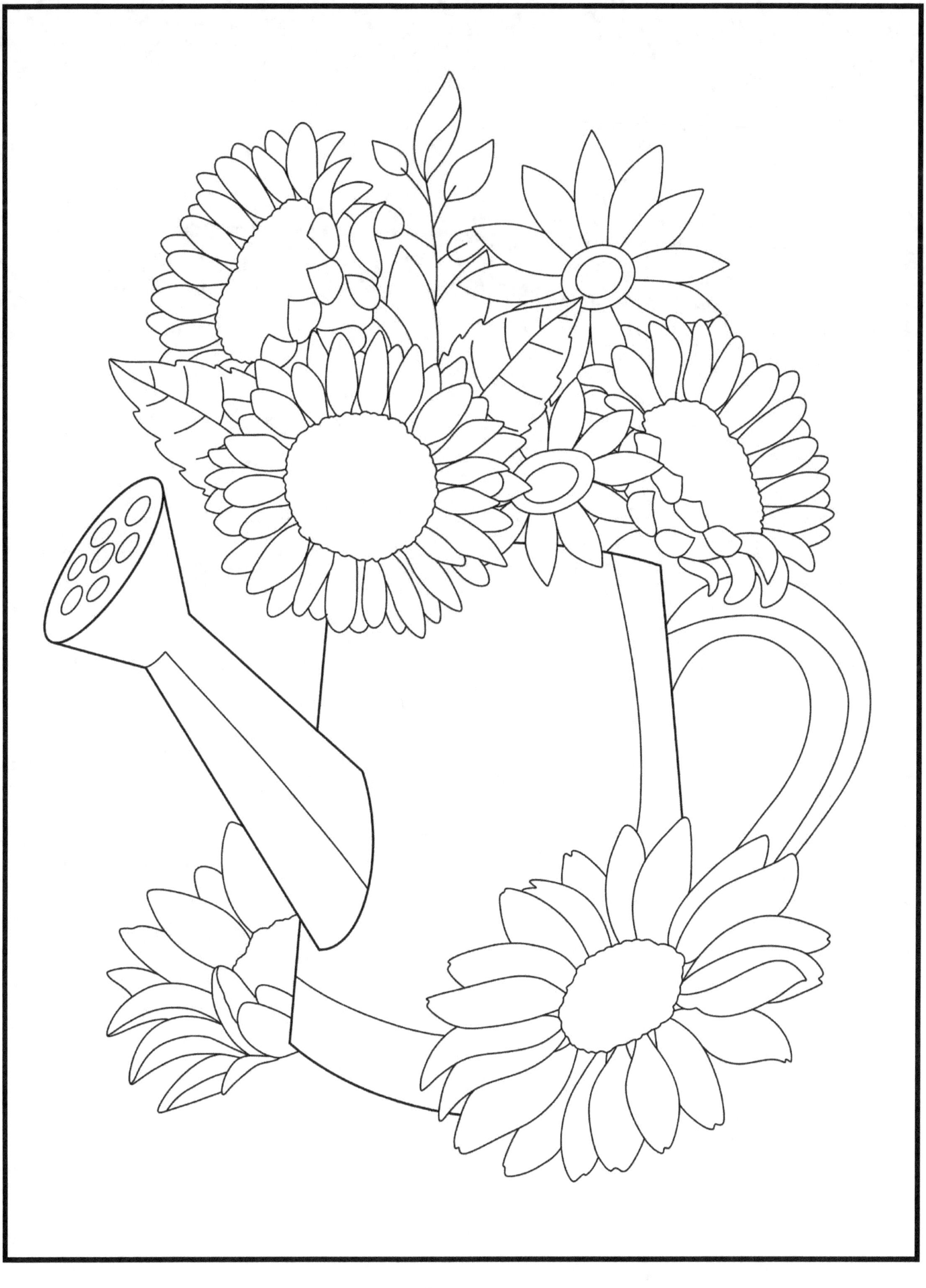

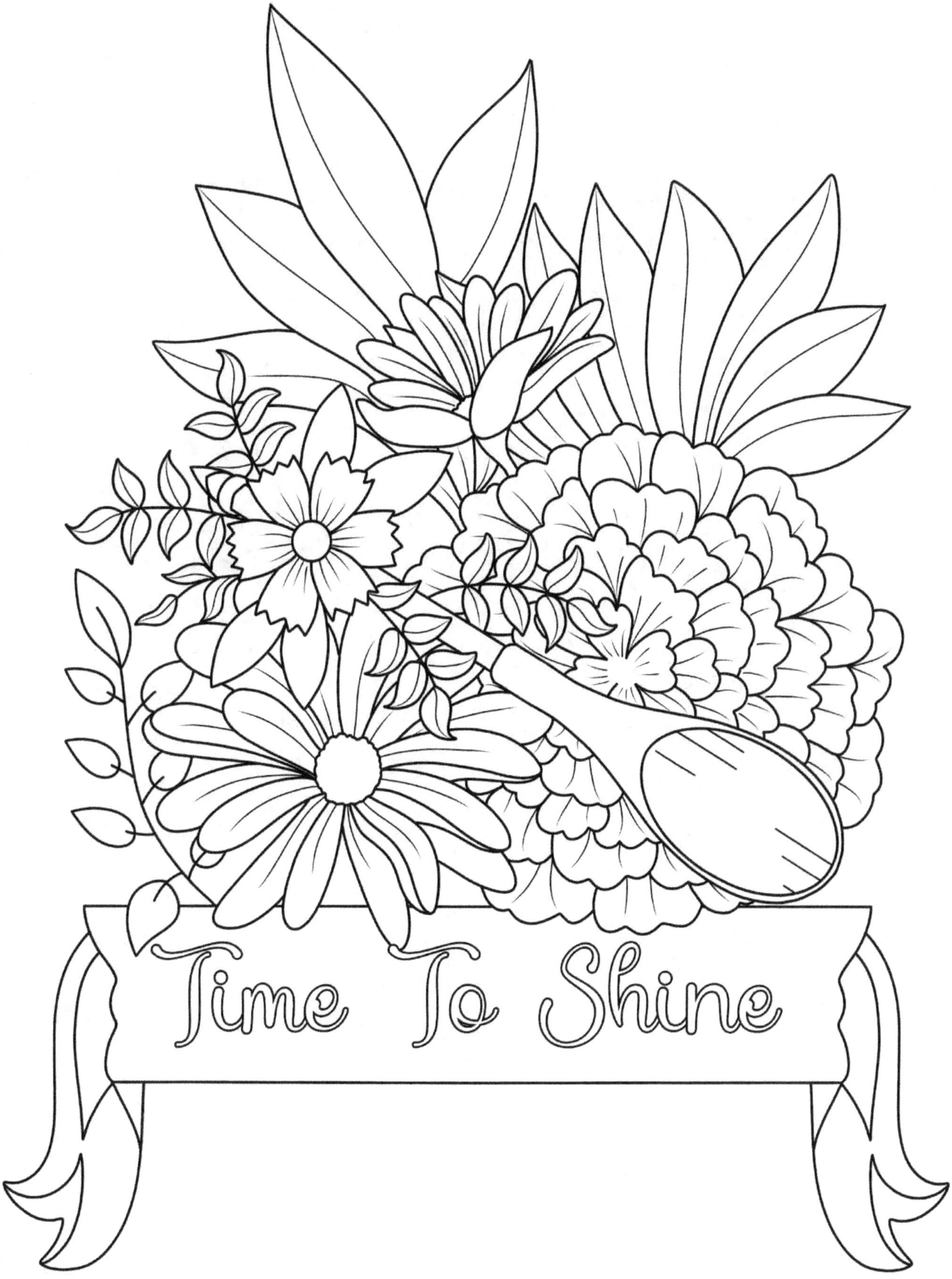
Time To Shine

www.ingramcontent.com/pod-product-compliance
Lightning Source LLC
Chambersburg PA
CBHW081744280726
48660CB00022B/3746